A PORTRAIT
OF THE
HORSE

ANDREW MORRIS & BOB LANGRISH

A PORTRAIT
OF THE
HORSE

ANDREW MORRIS & BOB LANGRISH

METRO BOOKS
NEW YORK

This 2007 edition published by
METRO BOOKS,
by arrangement with Regency House
Publishing Limited

Copyright ©2007 Regency House
Publishing Limited
Niall House
24–26 Boulton Road
Stevenage, Hertfordshire
SG1 4QX, UK

Metro Books
122 Fifth Avenue
New York, NY 10011

ISBN-13: 978-0-7607-9321-3

Printed and bound in Singapore

3 5 7 9 10 8 6 4 2

CONTENTS

INTRODUCTION 6

INTRODUCTION

It has taken nearly 60 million years for the horse to evolve from Eohippus, *the Dawn Horse, to the modern horse we know and love today. Horse-lovers do not need to be reminded of the debt they owe* Equus caballus, *but to others, this may not be so immediately apparent. While the horse has been eulogized and has on occasion even assumed mythical proportions, it is at heart a practical creature. While it has achieved harmony with mankind, it has never forgotten its place within the natural world.*

In a sense, the horse can be seen as man's traveling companion through life, and this is a task he has accepted with generosity and grace over many thousands of years. The horse, more than any other animal, has had the strongest connections with human history, and his influence on our culture has been profound. Before the dawning of the mechanical and industrial age, he was indispensable to man:
while he was sharing our lives on a domestic level, he was also a beast of burden and a method of transport. From carrying conquering armies into battle, he has made the seamless transition to his latest incarnation as an athlete, and now excels in sport and competition.

Wild horses were first domesticated in Eastern Europe and the Near East about 5,000 years ago, and by 1000 BC, could be found all over Europe, Asia and North Africa, all having evolved from three primeval types. These were Equus caballus sylvaticus, *the Forest Horse,* Equus caballus przewalskii *(the Asiatic Horse) and* Equus caballus gomellini, *the Tarpan, which exists as a protected species to this day.*

Indigenous prehistoric horses were once also present in the Americas, but one day they inexplicably disappeared and why this happened has never been discovered. It was the Spanish conquistadors who reintroduced their Iberian horses to the Americas and these continued to evolve in a different way from horses elsewhere. The early pioneers needed horses of great hardiness and stamina and their own horses evolved accordingly; bloodlines from other countries were later imported to improve and refine.

Today, modern breeding methods have produced the ultimate sporthorse. It is usually bred from coldblooded horses, such as Shires, crossed with hotbloods such as the Thoroughbred. These warmbloods are bred exclusively for sporting purposes, such as showjumping, eventing and dressage. They are not for work on the farm, but have been produced exclusively for people to enjoy and engage in competition. Well-known sporthorses include the Hanoverian, Trakhener, American Warmblood and Holstein.

A Portrait of the Horse *does not include every breed in existence today, but those that are featured all celebrate the strength and beauty of the horse through all its many guises.*

CHAPTER ONE

HORSES OF
THE AMERICAS

AMERICAN SADDLEBRED

The American Saddlebred was developed from horses originally brought to America from Europe in the 1600s, and particularly from Britain and what is now the Irish Republic. They had been used for trotting and pacing, and their hardy constitutions and extravagant paces made them popular in their new home.

The Narragansett Pacer, which was developed in Rhode Island in the 17th century, is believed to have been an ancestor of these European horses, and it was the model on which all easy-gaited horses in America were based thereafter.

Now extinct, the Pacer was noted for its docility and easy motion, making long days in the saddle more comfortable for the rider in the early days of the American colonies. Narragansett mares and Thoroughbred stallions were allowed to mate, with the result that the pacing gait and all-round ability were transferred to their offspring. Eventually, they were known as the American Horse, and when combined with Morgan, Standardbred and Thoroughbred blood, produced the American Saddlebred as it is known today.

While the traditional gaits of walk, trot and canter are innate, the Saddlebred is a breed apart, having inherited the ability to add additional gaits to its repertoire.

The American Saddlebred in capable not only of performing the usual gaits, but also of learning additional skills, such as the slow-stepping gait and the rack.

These include the slow gait or running walk, the stepping pace, and the slow rack, which is when both hooves on either side are in turn lifted almost simultaneously. This means that, at certain moments, all four hooves are off the ground, which is spectacular when combined with the horse's high-stepping action.

I will not change my horse with any that tread but on four pasterns . . . When I bestride him, I soar, I am a hawk. He trot the air, the earth sing when he touches it, the barest horn of his hoof is more musical than the pipe of Hermes.

William Shakespeare

This high-stepping carriage is sometimes falsely encouraged by keeping the feet long and building the feet up, while in other cases, the muscles under the dock are nicked to produce an unnaturally stiff and high tail-carriage: these are illegal practices in most countries of the world. The use of the tail brace also persists. This is sometimes fitted to a stabled horse in order that a high tail-carriage can be preserved; this, however, is at the expense of the horse's comfort when it is at rest. This practice should be modified or preferably banished if true recognition is to be achieved within the broader equestrian world.

The Saddlebred has a commanding presence and subtle expression of movement. The head is small and narrow, carried high, and the alert and intelligent expression is accentuated by the horse's fine pricked ears. The eyes are gentle but intelligent and the nose is straight with slightly flared nostrils. The neck is long and elegant and also carried high. The withers are high and run neatly into the back, which is fairly long, as is the barrel-shaped body. The shoulders are narrower at the top than the bottom and slope to create the trademark fluid action. The tail-carriage is naturally high, joined to flat quarters flowing into strong and powerful loins.

The Saddlebred is biddable and easy to train. It is gentle and affectionate, loves people, and enjoys being handled. At the same time, it is spirited and proud, with a keen intelligence and an alert demeanor. It tends to become excitable under saddle.

Saddlebreds come in all the usual solid colors, including palomino and roan, and there is often a good deal of white on the head and legs. The coat, mane and tail are fine and silky in texture. The horses typically range in size from 15–16.1hh.

Saddlebreds are highly prized within the show ring, particularly in the harness and ridden classes in which they excel; but they are also capable of competing in other events, performing equally well as dressage horses and showjumpers.

Colored Saddlebreds have been produced in recent years and are proving popular.

AMERICAN SHETLAND

As the name suggests, the American Shetland's ancestors were the native ponies of the Shetland Islands, situated off the northern coast of Scotland. In 1885, 75 ponies were imported to America by Eli Elliot, and were raised in the south-eastern states, where they thrived in spite of the warm, humid conditions. Their success led to the formation of the American Shetland Pony Club in 1888.

Today, the American Shetland is very different from its Scottish ancestor, being lighter in stature with longer, finer legs. This was achieved by crossing original Shetlands with small Arab, Thoroughbred and Hackney breeds, resulting in a small horse rather than a stock pony.

The American Shetland now excels in various driven classes, such as the two-wheeled roadster, four-wheeled buggy, and light sulky. It is also good with children and will happily compete in pony as well as breed classes and hunter-pony events. It is ridden in either English or Western tack.

It possesses all the showy attributes of its small horse ancestors, combined with the strength and workmanlike character of the Scottish original. The head is longish, nearer to that of a horse than a pony; the nose is straight, the ears fairly long, and the eyes are also more like those of a horse. It has retained many of the original Shetland's characteristics, in that mane and high-set tail are furnished with thick, strong hair. The

neck is quite short but the legs could be considered overlong, though they have retained their strength. The hooves retain the original Shetland strength and shape.

Having many of the attributes of the horse now in its make-up, the American Shetland has an equable temperament, and its small size makes it ideal for children to ride. It is reasonably hardy, making it easy to maintain.

American Shetlands come in all the usual solid colors, including roan, dun and cream. They sometimes achieve heights in the region of 11.2hh.

Bred to pull carts in ore and coal mines in the mid 1800s, American Shetlands have retained their driving ability. A well-trained Shetland not only excels at driving, but its classic maximum height of only 46 inches, makes it an excellent starter pony for a young child.

AMERICAN WARMBLOOD

The American Warmblood Registry was established to promote the breeding and enjoyment of American sporthorses. The organization has several major responsibilities, the first being to develop the breed to the highest standards in North America. This is achieved through careful maintenance of registries, studbooks and annual breeding-stock approvals. The organization also exists to serve its members and member breeders through marketing and education, which in turn promotes breeding of the highest possible standard.

The perfect American Warmblood is powerful and well-balanced, with plenty of good bone, making its gaits rhythmical and elastic. Its origination can be from a variety of bloodlines, as long as it has the qualities and talents to succeed. This will enable it to attain the required levels in traditional sports, such as dressage, showjumping and eventing, while at the same time remaining sound in mind and body.

American Warmbloods should appear uphill in action; they must also have a good conformation, in the sense of being well-proportioned and with good muscle tone. Temperament must be exemplary: the horse must be well-mannered and eager to impress, noble and attentive, and with a forward-thinking attitude.

American Warmbloods can be any color and are likely to achieve about 16.1hh in height.

I can always tell which is the front end of a horse, but beyond that, my art is not above the ordinary.

Mark Twain

The American Warmblood, in all its many forms, was bred to satisfy the demand for a high-quality sporthorse.

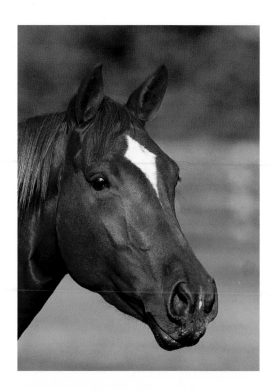

APPALOOSA

The gene that produces the many permutations of spots in horses is an ancient one, as indicated in Cro-Magnon depictions of such horses in cave paintings. For many centuries, spotted horses were highly prized in Europe and Asia and they were often featured in Chinese art.

The Spanish *conquistadores* brought their own such horses with them on their travels, introducing the spotted gene to the Americas when they arrived. After a time, some of these horses passed to Native Americans, in particular the Nez Percé, who lived in north-eastern Oregon, along the Palouse river. The Nez Percé, probably the first to introduce selective breeding, followed strict guidelines to produce the best results. They called this meeting of European and native stock the Appaloosa – possibly America's oldest breed.

Settlers eventually eliminated the Nez Percé, and the Appaloosa was dispersed throughout the land, the strain becoming weakened through random breeding.

Nowadays the Appaloosa is enjoying renewed popularity: it does not have to be spotted, however, although it is mandatory that other criteria be present: the Appaloosa must have sclera around the eyeballs, striped hooves, and mottled skin beneath the hair.

The Appaloosa is seen as the archetypal American horse. Developed from European and American bloodlines, it is popular as a versatile riding horse.

There are some obvious differences between American and European Appaloosas. The U.S. types have been crossed with Quarter Horses, with the result that their size and conformation are similar. In Europe, Appaloosas are rather larger, nearer to the size of a warmblood, making them ideal for jumping and dressage purposes. This type is also becoming popular in the United States.

The Appaloosa is a workmanlike horse, with a fairly plain head and short, tapered ears. The eyes are alert and inquisitive, with the mandatory white rings or sclera around the eyeball rims. The neck and body are compact and well-muscled and the quarters are powerful with well-developed limbs. The tail and mane hair is usually quite sparse. The hooves should be striped.

Appaloosas are great all-rounders: they are good-natured and hardy with plenty of stamina, speed and agility.

Color patterns include Blanket, which is a solid white area, normally over the quarters and loins, with a contrasting base color; Spots, when white or dark spots cover all or a portion of the body; Blanket with Spots, when there is a white blanket, with dark spots within the white area, usually in the same color as the base color; Roan, when a lighter-colored area develops on the face and over the back, loins and quarters; Roan Blanket with Spots, when there is a roan blanket which has white and/or dark spots within the roan area; Solid, when a base color has no contrasting color in the form of an Appaloosa coat pattern.

Appaloosas usually attain a height of between 14.2 and 15.2hh.

The Appaloosa is extremely versatile and looks good in Western tack. It is commonly used in Western events, such as roping, working cowhorse, and barrel-racing competitions. It is also used for showing, particularly in Britain, in riding horse and colored horse classes, and is proficient at cross-country and jumping.

AZTECA

The Azteca has now replaced the virtually extinct Mexican strain of Criollo horse and is one of the world's newest breeds. Work on the breed began in 1972, when three different bloodlines, Iberian (Andalusian or Lusitano), American Quarter Horse and Criollo were combined. The advantages of using these three breeds was to give the Azteca fine conformation, coupled with the hardiness and huge stamina of the Criollo. It also ensured that Mexican horse-breeding traditions were maintained.

The intention to avoid Thoroughbred or European warmblood types in the breeding was deliberate. The Azteca was intended to be an elegant riding horse with definite Spanish/Latin characteristics. It is a

horse that is useful for both leisure and for use in competition.

The Azteca's Spanish ancestry is obvious. The head is medium to small, with small alert ears and beautiful eyes with a touch of hauteur. The nose is either straight or slightly dished with large flaring nostrils. The neck is well-set, with plenty of muscle and an elegant arch; the shoulders are sloping with a medium-length body, strong, large quarters, and a slightly low-set tail. The legs are substantial with plenty of muscle and bone.

The Azteca has the noble mien of the Andalusian horse, the hardiness of the Criollo, and the speed, agility and amiability of the Quarter Horse. It can be any color other than piebald and skewbald. Aztecas stand between 14.3 and 15hh.

The Azteca is the happy result of a fusion of Spanish, American Quarter Horse, and Criollo bloodlines.

CRIOLLO

The Spanish conquistadors brought the horse to the Americas and they could have done nothing better than to introduce the Arab, Barb and excellent Iberian. It is these three bloodlines that went into the making of the Criollo, the native horse of Argentina. For many hundreds of years the Criollo roamed the treeless plains (pampas) of Argentina, where pitiless natural selection helped to form it into one of the toughest horses in the world.

Criollos eventually came to be ridden by gauchos, or South American cowboys, who also used them as packhorses, having quickly recognized their excellent hardiness, stamina, speed and resilience.

The Criollo is tough, can survive on next to nothing, and is an obedient worker. It is able to withstand some of the harshest conditions in the world.

Today, herds live in a semi-wild condition on the enormous ranches of South America, where they are caught and broken in as required. They are still used

These days, the Criollo is becoming something of a rarity, Fortunately, steps are being taken to protect the breed.

as stock and riding horses, and they make excellent polo ponies when crossed with Thoroughbreds.

Rigorous endurance tests to evaluate Criollos for breeding are used where horses ride over a 466-mile (750-km) course, carrying a load of 245lb (111kg), to be completed in a set time. During this time, the horses feed only on what they

can forage for themselves, and they are checked by veterinarians when the test has been completed.

The Criollo's toughness is more than obvious from its stocky exterior. The head is broad with wide-set eyes and the nose is slightly dished. It has fairly large ears. The neck is well-developed with a wide back and chest and strong quarters. The back is also short, with sloping shoulders, and the short, sturdy legs possess plenty of bone.

Color is most commonly dun, with a black mane and tail, an eel stripe down the center of the back, and zebra markings on the legs. Other colors are chestnut, bay, black, roan, gray, piebald, skewbald and palomino. Height is from 14–15hh.

FALABELLA

It is said that the Falabella's ancestors were first seen in the 19th century, in among the herds of South American Indians. But it was more probably the creation of the Falabella family, at their ranch near Buenos Aires in Argentina, over a century ago. The breed was established by first crossing small Arab and Thoroughbred stallions with Shetland Pony mares. Then, using selective breeding, it was made ever smaller.

The Falabella is not a pony: it is a miniature horse with all the conformation and character of a horse. Because of excessive in-breeding, however, the

The tiny Falabella is not classified as a pony, but is in fact a small horse, capable of being ridden only by very small children.

conformation of some individuals is far from ideal, consequently they tend to look rather odd. They are also weak for their size and can be ridden only by the smallest children. Today, breeders are attempting to rectify these faults and are generally trying to improve the breed.

Being affectionate, Falabellas make ideal pets and are sometimes allowed even into peoples' homes because of their small size. They are popular in special in-hand showing classes and can pull small carts.

Correctly bred, a Fallabella should resemble a miniature Thoroughbred or Arab, though its Shetland ancestry may occasionally come to the fore. The head is refined and horse-like, with a straight nose and small, flared nostrils. The small ears are set wide apart, and the eyes are kind. The body is medium-length, with a slim frame, and the legs are fine, similar to those of a Thoroughbred.

The Falabella is a delightful breed. It provides all the pleasures of a larger breed but at a lower cost; this is particularly true as far as land requirements are concerned. However, its constitution is less that robust and it requires the same care that one would give to any finely-bred horse. It is amenable, docile and obedient.

Falabellas come in all solid colors, as well as gray and roan, and Appaloosa markings are also common. Ideally, they should stand no taller than 30in (76cm) from the ground.

FLORIDA CRACKER

Florida cowboys, nicknamed 'crackers', because of the sound made by their whips as they cracked them in the air, passed the same name on to their small, agile horses. The horses were descended from Spanish stock, dating from the 1500s, when the Spaniard, Juan Ponce de Leon, on his second Florida trip, brought horses, cattle and other livestock to the Americas.

Florida Crackers were fairly common until the beginning of the 20th century, but during the 1930s their decline gathered pace, and before long, the breed was on the edge of extinction. By the late 1980s, only a few small herds, owned and bred by ranching families, remained. Fortunately, the ranchers recognized their importance.

The Cracker, with its proven abilities as a cowhorse, is a quick, hardy animal that is easy to ride. The breed has changed very little over the years and it is much the same as it was at the time of the Spanish

conquistadors, more than 500 years ago.

Today numbers are rising, and though still not plentiful, the demand for the breed is continuing to grow. New breeding herds have been established and the importance of the Cracker to Florida's heritage is now thankfully recognized. The Florida Cracker Horse Association was chartered in April 1989 to preserve and perpetuate the horse as a unique Spanish colonial breed.

The Florida Cracker is a small saddle horse, ranging in height from 13.2 to 15 hh. They are short in the back, and have a sloping rump. They can be of any colour, although grays are more common.

Once in jeopardy, the Florida Cracker's future is at last looking more promising, now that it has been recognized as an important part of Florida's living history.

GALICEÑO

The Galiceño is a descendant of the Galician horses of north-western Spain and the Garrano mountain ponies of Portugal. It was among the horses brought with him to the Americas by the Spanish conquistador, Hernando Cortes, when he invaded Mexico in 1519.

Once in Mexico, some of these horses are thought to have been stolen by the native population, or they may simply have escaped, but they were left to roam in a semi-wild state, when the breed developed through natural selection. Eventually, they

He knows when you're happy
He knows when you're comfortable
He knows when you're confident
And he always knows when you
have carrots.

Anon.

came to be regarded as almost indigenous to the continent.

There is much of the Arab horse in the Galiceño's bloodline, and many of the fine characteristics of the breed have been inherited. Galiceños are popular in North America as children's riding ponies and do

well in children's competitions. In Latin America, however, they are still used as workhorses on ranches, where strength and stamina is particularly important.

The Galiceño is capable of carrying a man over rugged terrain for a day without tiring. It has an ususual gait, known as a 'running walk,' which enables it to cover ground quickly, efficiently and smoothly, making it ideal for riding and for showing in harness.

Small and compact, the Galiceño's Arab ancestry is noticeable in the fine, narrow head. It has thin pointed ears, a small muzzle, and large, flaring nostrils. The

eyes are large and intelligent, and the neck is long and well-developed, with a long, full mane. The withers are prominent, with a good sloping shoulder and a deep girth. The body is quite stocky, but the back is unusually narrow. Unlike the Arab, the tail is set low and, like the mane, it is allowed to grow long. Though fine, the legs are strong, with well-shaped hard hooves.

The Galiceño is comfortable to ride over a long period because of its long, smooth gait. Its intelligence and quick reactions also make it excellent in competition.

Standing between 12 and 13.2hh, it comes with all the usual solid coat colors, including palomino, dun and gray. Part-coloreds or albinos, however, are not permitted.

Originally the product of Spanish Galician and Portuguese Garrano bloodlines, the Galiceño also owes a legacy to the Arab horse, which has contributed greatly to the attractiveness of the breed.

MANGALARGA MARCHADOR

Brazil and Portugal have been closely connected for centuries, and at one time even had the same ruler, Don João VI, in around 1815. It was he who was responsible for bringing quality Portuguese and Spanish horses to Brazil, particularly the Andalusian and the Altér Real.

The Brazilian Mangalarga is a direct descendant of one particular Altér Real stallion, which was mated with Criollo mares, though more Altér Real, Barb and Andalusian were eventually added to improve the breed. The result is neat, lightly-built, and strongly reminiscent of the Barb, but with the rolling gait of the Spanish breeds.

The Mangalarga is most often used on the enormous estancias of Brazil, where its fifth gait, known as the *marcha*, makes it fast but comfortable to ride. It has a

smooth, stable walk, canter and gallop, as well as a natural diagonal (*batida*) or lateral (*picada*) four-beat gait.

The Mangalarga's head is high and proud, with medium-length ears, intelligent eyes, and a nose that is straight with flaring nostrils. The back is long with strong loins and neat quarters; the shoulders are sloping with a deep girth, and there are well-muscled legs with hard hooves.

The Mangalarga has incredible stamina, and this enables it to work all day and cover huge distances. It is good-natured, willing and obedient. Coat colors are usually bay, gray, chestnut and roan. Height is around 15hh.

Today, the Mangalarga Marchador is also used for endurance and trail-riding, jumping and polo. It is an excellent and versatile riding and showing horse.

MISSOURI FOX TROTTER

The Missouri Fox Trotter was developed in the 19th century by settlers in Missouri and Arkansas. Initially, its purpose was to be a general riding horse, with the speed and endurance to cope with difficult terrain. The foundation stock for the breed was the Morgan, which was infused with Thoroughbred and Arab as well as Iberian blood.

As horses with elaborate gaits became more popular, the breed was later mated with the Saddlebred and Tennessee Walking Horse, which greatly improved its elegance, bearing and paces, including its foxtrot gait; this is basically a diagonal gait, like the

The Missouri Fox Trotter is named for its extra foxtrot gait.

trot, in which the horse appears to be walking with the front legs while trotting with the hind.

In the early days, before racing was made illegal, the Fox Trotter had been a useful competitor, but after the ban it reverted to its use as a general riding horse.

A stud book for the breed was eventually opened in 1948. The breed society, however, put in place strict guidelines that the Missouri Fox Trotter should have no artificial aids to influence and enhance its gait, such as nicking or setting the tail; consequently its action is not as pronounced or extravagant as the

American Saddlebred, for example. The breed is popular in the United States, where it is used for general riding, showing and endurance.

The head is a little plain, with a straight nose and a square muzzle with large open nostrils. The ears are medium-length and alert and the eyes have a kind but intelligent expression. The neck is medium-length and fairly well-developed, with prominent withers; the back is short, with strong loins and hindquarters. The tail is set fairly low, and the legs are long with large joints and well-shaped, strong hooves.

The Missouri Fox Trotter has a charming, easy-going manner. It is willing and obedient with excellent stamina and endurance. It comes in colors and can be part-colored and stands from 14–16hh.

MORGAN

One of America's most famous and versatile breeds, all Morgans can be traced back to just one stallion called Figure. Figure was later renamed Justin Morgan after its owner, Thomas Justin Morgan, a tavern keeper and singing teacher who supplemented his income by breeding stallions.

The colt was born in around 1790 in Vermont. It is thought that its sire was probably a Welsh Cob, called True Briton,

The Morgan is one of the first breeds ever to have been developed in the United States.

though little is known of the dam, other than that she may have had Oriental and Thoroughbred blood.

Thomas Justin Morgan was so impressed with his stallion's looks and personality, that he eventually decided to put him to stud. The results were remarkable: it did not matter what mare Justin Morgan covered, a foal the image of its father was produced. Moreover, the sire's prowess as a marvellous harness and riding horse seemed to have been replicated in the offspring, the performance of each of them being second to none. In fact, all were amazed that such a significant and impressive breed could have developed from a single stallion.

Morgans are just as versatile today – used in harness competitions, shows, driving and trail-riding. They are strong and hard-working, and have a spirited but tractable nature.

The head should provide immediate evidence of quality, with beautiful and expressive eyes. The muzzle is small and the profile straight or slightly dished. The neck is well-crested and the shoulders strong. The hindquarters are large and strong and the legs sturdy.

A type known as the Park Morgan is bred particularly for its high-stepping action. Another type is the Pleasure Morgan, whose action is less exaggerated. All solid colors are acceptable in this breed. They stand somewhere between 14 and 15.2hh.

The Morgan is an attractive breed, and excels in all areas of equitation.

MUSTANG

Although horses had once been present in North America, by the time the conquistadors arrived in the 16th century, the original prehistoric horses had long been extinct. The Spanish brought Iberian horses with them in their ships, derived mainly from Arabs and Barbs. Many of these sleek, desert-bred and resilient horses were allowed to wander off, spreading into North America and forming feral herds. They became known as Mustangs.

Native American tribes came to value the Mustang's qualities and many were caught and domesticated by them. They even developed their own breeds based on the Mustang, such as the Appaloosa, the Cayuse Indian Pony and the Chickasaw Indian Pony, also known as the Florida Cracker Horse.

There were between one- and two-million Mustangs in existence by the beginning of the 19th century, many of them still running free, though others had been caught and were being used by settlers. Unfortunately, the wild horses

Today, the herds of feral Mustangs are shadows of their former selves, but efforts are now being made to protect the breed.

came to be regarded as pests, and were culled in their thousands to make way for cattle. It was not only the ranchers who were responsible for their decimation, thousands were also killed in the 20th century, sacrificed to the pet-food industry.

Sadly, there are less than 50,000 Mustangs in existence today and in some areas numbers are dangerously low.

A PORTRAIT OF THE HORSE

A thousand horse and none to ride! -
With flowing tail, and flying mane,
Wide nostrils never stretched by pain,
Mouths bloodless to the bit or rein,
And feet that iron never shod,
And flanks unscarred by spur or rod,
A thousand horse, the wild, the free,
Like waves that follow o'er the sea,
Came thickly thundering on...

Lord Byron

Determined efforts are now being made to safeguard the breed for the future and, fortunately for the Mustang, the breed is

now seen as an important part of the American heritage and a protected species.

Mustangs come in all colors, sizes and builds, although horses that display Barb characteristics are particularly favored by breeders. The Mustang is easy to train, due to its innate intelligence, and it is tough and resilient. It can be any color, although it is mainly brown, chestnut, bay or dun. Its height varies from 14–16hh.

Young Mustangs are relatively easy to domesticate and make excellent riding horses.

45

NATIONAL SHOW HORSE

The National Show Horse is a relatively new breed, founded in 1981. It is a cross between an American Saddlebred and an Arabian, but various crosses will be used to improve the breed. Stallions are carefully selected and must themselves be pure-bred, and each stallion has to be approved by the NSHR board of directors. Registered offspring must contain from 25 to 99 per cent Arab blood.

This is a horse of outstanding elegance and beauty. It has the striking looks of the Saddlebred and the classical beauty of the Arabian. It has the long, high-set neck of

The elegant National Show Horse may be of any solid color, or it may be part-colored like the horses on the right.

The National Show Horse displays the best attributes of both the American Saddlebred and the Arabian horse.

the Saddlebred, which should not have a pronounced crest, but be more like that of a swan. The head must be small and refined, and the ears must also be small. The profile should be straight or slightly concave. The National Show Horse is a short-coupled horse, with a deep, laid-back shoulder. The tail should always be carried high. The cannon bones are long in front and the pasterns are long and sloping.

The flashy park horse is suitable for saddle seat riding. It has a high-stepping action and a very elevated front end. In general, the breed can be used for a variety of disciplines, including endurance, jumping, dressage and Western riding. It is even-tempered and appears to be comfortable around people, being naturally friendly, lively and energetic. Any coat color is permitted. In height it stands somewhere between 15.2 and 16.2hh.

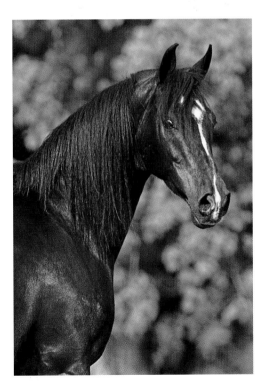

PASO FINO

Coming from Puerto Rico, the foundation of the Paso Fino is old Spanish or Iberian stock. It has the same bloodlines, inherited from horses brought to the Americas by the Spanish conquistadors in the 16th century; however, in terms of character and conformation, different environments have caused slight variations in their evolution.

The Paso Fino is a naturally gaited horse, like the Peruvian Paso or Stepping Horse (page 52), and another lesser-known Colombian breed, and although it is predominantly a working horse, these attributes make it stand out from the crowd. Aficionados claim that because of its natural, even, four-beat gait, that can be performed at varying speeds, it is the smoothest riding horse in the world. The classic *fino* is a collected gait, executed with a rapid footfall that covers little ground. The *paso corto* is a moderate gait, useful in trail

Ancient Iberian bloodlines are still very much in evidence in the Paso Fino.

riding, and the *paso largo* is a fast gait in which the horse can reach speeds equivalent to a canter or slow gallop. Not all Paso Finos can perform the classic *fino*, but the majority perform the other gaits with ease.

There are another two variants: the *sobre paso*, a more natural gait in which the horse is allowed a loose rein and is relaxed, and which is used in general riding rather than the show ring; and the *andadura*, which is a fast, pacing gait. This is uncomfortable, however, so it is only performed for short periods. The rest of the time the horse's

effortless gait makes riding it extremely comfortable and smooth.

Paso Finos are in great demand for showing and displays. The head is fine, almost Arab-like, with a straight nose and flaring nostrils. It has longish, well-shaped ears and intelligent eyes. The body is very Spanish, similar to the Andalusian's, with a good sloping shoulder, well-developed neck, and a medium-length back. It has slightly sloping quarters and a low-set tail. The legs are sturdy and strong with large hocks.

The Paso Fino has an excellent temperament and great enthusiasm. Despite its small stature it is very strong; in fact, even the smallest will easily carry a man over hills and rough terrain. They may be any color and stand between 14 and 15hh.

He's of the colour of the nutmeg. And of the heat of the ginger.... he is pure air and fire; and the dull elements of earth and water never appear in him, but only in patient stillness while his rider mounts him; he is indeed a horse, and all other jades you may call beasts.

William Shakespeare

PERUVIAN PASO

As its name suggests, the Peruvian Paso, or Peruvian Stepping Horse, comes from Peru. It shares much of its descent with the Paso Fino, the national horse of Puerto Rico, the foundation of both breeds being Barb and old Spanish or Iberian stock brought to the Americas by the conquistadors in the 16th century.

The Peruvian Paso has adapted well to its environment and is able to carry riders great distances over dangerous mountain terrain with safety and comfort. It has also adapted to the high altitudes of the Andes Range and has a larger, stronger heart and greater lung capacity than other breeds; this enables it to function energetically in areas where oxygen is scarce.

Like the other Paso breeds, the Peruvian has the natural ability to perform the attractive four-beat lateral gaits that make riding long distances so comfortable for the rider without tiring the horse. There are three gaits: the *paso corto*, used for practical purposes; the *paso fino*, an exaggerated slow gait used in the show ring and in parades, which has the appearance almost of slow motion; and the *paso largo*, which is fast. These traits are passed from mare to foal and are completely natural, needing no artificial aids. Once a person becomes accustomed to the gaits (the horse never trots or gallops) the Peruvian makes an excellent riding horse.

In stature, the Peruvian is similar to its cousin the Paso Fino. The head is fine and resembles that of the Barb, with shapely pricked ears and a proud, alert look. The nostrils are readily dilated, presumably to allow as much oxygen as possible to be taken in. The body has all the evidence of a Spanish inheritance and is similar to the Andalusian's. The legs are sturdy, quite long, and well-muscled with hard hooves.

The Peruvian Paso shares much of its ancestry with the Paso Fino, including its extravagant gaits.

While the Peruvian Paso is hardy and energetic, it is also even-tempered and intelligent. It is an obedient and willing worker. Peruvians may be any color, but bay or chestnut, with white on the head and legs, is permitted. The mane and tail are abundant, with fine, lustrous hair that may be straight or curly. They range in height between 14 and 15.2hh.

PINTO/PAINT HORSE

The Pinto or Paint Horse (from the Spanish *pintado*, meaning 'painted'), like many of the old American breeds, is descended from Iberian horses, that were brought to the Americas by the conquistadors in the 16th century. They are sometimes referred to as 'calico' horses in America.

Paints are useful horses when it comes to trail-riding, being sure-footed and with plenty of stamina.

In England and other anglophone countries they are referred to as 'piebalds' (black-and-white) or 'skewbalds' (any other color and white) because their coats, of any solid color, are heavily mottled with white; alternatively they are merely referred to as colored horses, though in the United States the Pinto is regarded as a separate breed.

The original Spanish horses were allowed to revert to a feral condition and gradually extended into North America, where they roamed the Western deserts. Once domesticated by Native Americans,

When you're young and you fall off a horse, you may break something. When you're my age, you splatter.

Roy Rogers

however, they became greatly revered; in fact, it was believed that the Pinto even possessed magic powers.

Ranchers also adopted these hardy horses, whose stamina and agility made them excellent for work over great distances. Today they are still used as workhorses but also at rodeos; they are

also used for trail-riding and showing and as all-round riding horses.

The Pinto has a fine head and graceful, well-defined neck. The ears are alert and of medium length, while the eyes indicate spirit and intelligence. They are usually quite short in the back, with long, strong legs and hard, tough hooves. They are hardy and agile.

The Pinto is well-known for its striking coat, which can be black, chestnut, brown, bay, dun, sorrel, palomino, gray or roan, patched with large areas of white. There are three distinctive types of coat pattern: Tobiano, in which the head is like that of any solid-colored horse, but there are round

The Paint horse's three most distinctive coat patterns are Tobiano, Overo and Tovero.

or oval spots resembling shields running over the neck and chest. One or both flanks may be colored white or a color can predominate, while the tail is often bi-colored; Overo, which is predominantly dark or white, though the white shouldn't cross the back between withers and tail. The head should be white with scattered irregular markings on the rest of the body. At least one leg should be dark and the tail is usually one color; Tovero is a mixture of the two. Pintos stand between 14.2 and 15.2hh.

PONY OF THE AMERICAS

This is a relatively new breed dating from the 1950s and is the result of an accidental cross between a Scottish Shetland Pony and an Appaloosa mare with Arab connexions. When the foal, Black Hand I, was born, it was found to be a smaller version of its dam and it was this stallion that became the foundation of America's first pony breed.

The breed has the appearance of a small horse rather than a pony; later on, further refinement was added when Quarter Horse and Arab bloodlines were introduced, producing the showy, high-stepping action so popular in the show ring today.

Leslie Boomhower, an Iowa breeder of Shetland Ponies, is regarded as the founder of the Pony of the Americas breed.

Similar in stature to British Thoroughbred ponies, the Pony of the Americas is ideal for small children, who find it easy to handle. It is also strong enough to carry a small adult and is used in

endurance, trail-riding and showjumping, as well as trotting and pony flat-racing.

The head is very Arab, with a broad forehead, small pricked ears, and a straight or slightly dished nose. The eyes are large and kind. The body is of medium length, with a good sloping shoulder, well-developed quarters, and fine but strong legs. It is strong and hardy, with a calm but willing disposition. It shares similar markings with the Appaloosa, and stands between 11.2 and 14hh.

I heard a neigh. Oh, such a brisk and melodious neigh as that was! My very heart leaped with delight at the sound.

Nathaniel Hawthorne

QUARTER HORSE

It is no surprise that the Quarter Horse holds pride of place in the hearts of all American horse-lovers, seeing that it was the first breed to become established in the United States.

The Quarter Horse's origins can be traced back 500 years to the time when the Spanish conquistadors brought Iberian and Oriental horses to Florida. English colonists eventually acquired these horses from Chickasaw Indians, which they crossed with their own English horses, mainly Thoroughbreds, then refined them again with more Thoroughbred blood.

Before the days of race tracks, the early colonists used to race their horses down the main street, which was usually about a quarter-of-a-mile long. The name Quarter

The Quarter Horse excels on the race track, but also makes a good general riding horse.

Horse, therefore, came from the ability of these horses to achieve great speeds over a short distance. The powerful hindquarters of the Quarter Horse gave it great acceleration and even today it is faster than the Thoroughbred over short sprints.

The Quarter Horse was not only a talented sprinter, it also made a good riding horse, pulled wagons, and was an efficient packhorse. However, its most valuable attribute was its natural instinct to round up herds. This undoubtedly had been inherited from its Iberian forebears, which had nerves of steel and amazing agility. They also had plenty of cow sense, having worked the bullrings of Portugal and Spain for generations. Today, however, racing predominates, but their use in rodeos, trailing and as all-round family mounts is widespread across the United States, Canada, Australia and even parts of Europe.

Quarter Horses can be quite large animals, due to the influence of the Thoroughbred in their breeding. The head is relatively small and the eyes are bright and set far apart. The neck, hindquarters and back are extremely muscular, which makes the feet appear relatively small.

There are two distinct types of Quarter Horse – the old-fashioned original or 'bulldog' type, and the 'racing Quarter', which is nearer in looks to a well-muscled Thoroughbred.

Quarter Horses are easy to maintain, and are enthusiastic, honest and energetic. Their coats may be of any color, and their height range is between 14.2 and 16hh.

STANDARDBRED

The Standardbred is famous for its trotting and pacing abilities and is widely used in harness racing throughout the world. The breed dates back 200 years, when trotting races had become sufficiently popular to warrant a breeding program of their own.

The founding sire of today's Standardbred was Messenger, a gray Thoroughbred, born in 1780 and imported to Philadelphia in 1788. While Messenger was bred for traditional racing at a gallop, his own sire, Mambrino, had been responsible for a long dynasty of famous trotting coachhorses in England.

Messenger worked at stud for about 20 years and became famous for producing strong, talented trotters. Meanwhile, during the mid-1800s in New England, the Morgan breed was being used to produce a

Standardbreds are so called because only horses that could race a mile in a standard time or better could be registered. The Standardbred stud book was opened in 1939.

line of smaller trotters with a straight up-and-down action. The high-stepping action of the Morgan line was then combined with the long-reaching stride of the Messenger, which increased the performance of the Standardbred no end.

The trot of a Standardbred appears huge in comparison with that of ordinary breeds and is a gait whereby the legs are moved in diagonal pairs. However, the 'pace' is peculiar to this breed and is a gait where the horse moves its legs in lateral pairs. While the trot comes naturally to all

Horse sense is the thing a horse has which keeps it from betting on people.

W.C. Fields

horses, the pace generally has to be taught, although some Standardbreds seem to be able to pace from birth. Pacing is quicker than trotting as it allows the stride to be longer and more economical.

The term Standardbred was introduced in 1879 and derives from the

time standard that was set to test the ability of harness racers. Originally, the Standardbred horse was required to cover a mile in 2 minutes and 30 seconds. Since this first standard was set, improved breeding has enabled the modern Standardbred to beat this target easily.

The head is in proportion to the horse's body and the eyes are kind, while the ears are indicative of its alertness. The horse is muscular overall, with a well-sprung barrel, sloping shoulder, and a strong back. The legs resemble those of the Thoroughbred, though they are rather

Because of their skill, Standardbreds are often used to upgrade other breeds of harness racers around the world.

more solid, with larger joints; the hooves are large and strong.

The Standardbred has an excellent temperament and is quite a placid horse when away from the race track. When racing, however, it is highly competitive, and displays great stamina and unbounding energy. They come in all solid colors, but mainly bay, black, brown and chestnut. Size ranges from 14.2–17.2hh.

TENNESSEE WALKING HORSE

The Tennessee (or Plantation) Walking Horse originated in the deep south of the United States and was recognized as the ideal utility breed to carry plantation owners around their large estates. The smooth, gliding gait of the 'Walker' (as the breed is also known) provided hours of comfort in the saddle; the movement is performed from the elbow rather than the shoulder, thus transmitting the minimum of movement to the rider. Although still widely ridden for pleasure, the Walker is nowadays extensively bred for the show ring, and it is also used as a general riding and harness horse.

In fact there are two or three characteristic gaits, the flat-footed walk, the running walk, and the canter. The first horse perceived to have this natural talent was foaled in 1837, but it took another 50 years or so to establish the breed as it is today.

The Thoroughbred, Standardbred, American Saddlebred, Narragansett Pacer and Morgan bloodlines all played their part in establishing this distinctive breed, but it was one stallion, born in 1886, that became its foundation stallion. It possessed all the desired qualities, such as the delightful temperament and the characteristic gaits. Nearly all of the offspring inherited their sire's traits and he subsequently enjoyed many successful years at stud. Once a breed association had become well-established, approximately 300,000 horses were registered.

The Walker has a large head with a straight profile, gentle eyes, and pointed ears. The neck is arched and muscular, with a broad base that enables the head to be carried elegantly high. The breed has plenty of bone, which adds to its sturdiness, and a short-coupled and level topline. The limb

The Tennessee Walker is frequently to be seen in programs featuring handicapped riders, and people with back problems often find it a more comfortable horse to ride.

joints are well-made, with particularly powerful hocks that allow the hindlegs to step well under the body. The tail, which is usually left long, is often nicked and set artificially high.

Walkers are naturally gentle and calm, but it is their unusual gaits for which they are most famous. Although the gaits are inherited, they need to be developed by further training. The flat walk, running walk and canter are natural to the breed. The running walk has several variations: the rack, the stepping pace, the fox-trot and single-foot.

They may be any color, but especially black, chestnut, brown, gray, roan or bay. Height is between 15 and 17hh.

CHAPTER TWO

HORSES OF EUROPE

ALTÉR REAL

Portugal has two breeds of horses, both of which are used in the bullring and in *haute école* classical riding: the famous Lusitano (page 166) and the lesser known but no less noble, Altér Real. The breed had its beginnings in the 18th century, when 300 Andalusian mares, intended for the specific requirements of the Portuguese court in Lisbon, were brought from Jerez in Spain to the royal house of Braganza's

stud at Vila de Portel in Portugal. After eight years, the stud moved to Altér do Chão, which gave the horse the first part of its name, the second part meaning royal. For many years the breed excelled not only at classical disciplines but also as a quality carriage horse.

The Altér Real breed came under jeopardy during the Napoleonic invasion of 1809–10, when troops stole the best horses from the stud, drastically reducing their numbers. Then, in 1832, King Miguel

The Altér Real is termed a Baroque horse, being particularly suited to haute école classicism.

abdicated and much of the stud's land became subject to confiscation.

In later years, measures were taken to improve the existing stock by breeding it with Thoroughbreds, Normans and Arabs; this, however, only served to weaken the breed, causing much loss of its original character. In the late 19th century, however,

The head has all the distinctive Iberian qualities of the Lusitano and Andalusian, having a fine head with a slightly dished nose, medium-length shapely ears, and a lively, intelligent eye. The neck is short but well-positioned, with a pronounced, arched crest. The shoulders are sloping and the chest is well-developed. The back is short and strong with ample quarters. The legs are hard and very tough, the upper parts being well-muscled with large joints, ending in small but well-shaped hooves.

The Altér Real has a high-stepping action which is most attractive: this, coupled with its strength and power, makes it appear much larger than it actually is. Unlike its Iberian brothers, the Altér Real is not suitable for beginners as it has inherited a fiery and lively temperament from non-Iberian blood added in the early 19th century. It is responsive and learns quickly but needs a competent and experienced rider in order to excel. Coat color is usually bay and height is between 15 and 16hh.

the Spanish Zapata family introduced more Andalusian and Carthusian blood, and this reversed much of the earlier damage.

The breed finally obtained the protection it deserved in the early 20th century, when steps were taken to restore it to its former glory. This was achieved with the help of Dr. Ruy d'Andrade who, with two stallions and a handful of mares, founded a top-quality Altér Real stud. He eventually handed the stud over to the Portuguese Ministry of Agriculture, which administers the breeding program today. The Altér Real is still used in *haute école* and general riding.

Even though it has a more famous equine compatriot in the Lusitano, the Altér Real is considered to be Portugal's national horse.

ANDALUSIAN

This celebrated Spanish breed is one of the oldest to have been handled and ridden by man: there is further evidence of this fact in cave paintings, which confirm that horses of this kind were present in the Iberian Peninsula around 5,000 BC.

The Andalusian's lineage stems from the Sorraia Pony, which still exists in Iberia, and the North African Barb, with additional Arab and Oriental strains. It evolved in Iberia, most of which was then known as Andalusia, at the time of the Moorish occupation of 711. The result was a horse with a head-carriage that was high and proud, and paces that were extravagant and highly-placed.

The Andalusian was particularly valued as a warhorse, having all the qualities that enabled it to perform well in battle. (It is interesting to note that El Cid's mount, Babieca, was an Andalusian.) Later, in the 16th century, the conquistadors brought the horse with them to the Americas, where it became the basis of all American breeds.

The Andalusian bloodline is evident in around 80 per cent of modern breeds and has had a particular influence on the Connemara, native to Ireland, the Lipizzaner of the Balkans, and the Cleveland Bay and Welsh Cob of the British Isles. This also applies to American breeds,

A horse is worth more than riches.

Spanish Proverb

The Andalusian is one of the purest breeds of horses present in the world today. It shares similarities with the closely-related Lusitano breed.

which also share lineage with the Lusitano, Carthusian, and Altér Real.

But this popularity was not to last, and in around 1700 the Andalusian's heavy, robust conformation fell from favor, when lighter, sleeker animals, used for hunting and racing, became more fashionable. Andalusians suffered even more when a plague and famine almost wiped them out; a few survived in the Carthusian monasteries of Castello, Jerez and Seville, where breeding from the best of the animals continued.

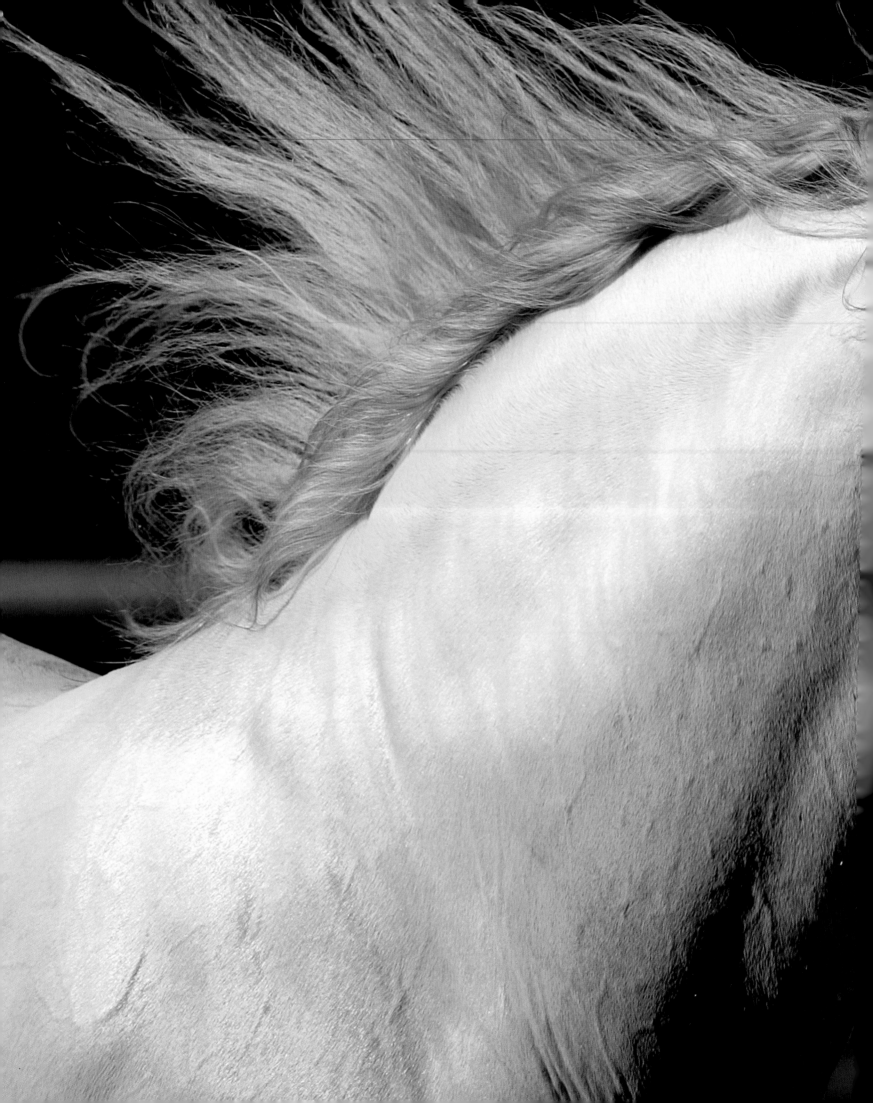

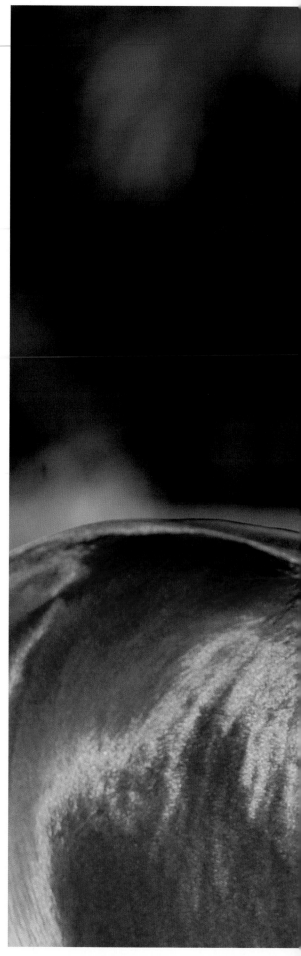

Today's Andalusian can still be traced back to these lines, the purest and most beautiful of which are still referred to as *caballos Cartujanos*. Their extreme rarity forced the Spanish government to ban their export for over 100 years, but the embargo was lifted in the 1960s, and they now enjoy popularity around the world.

Today the Andalusian is used for bullfighting and display riding, where its power and agility allow it to execute the intricate movements with ease. They excel at advanced classical dressage and at showjumping and are also useful for general riding and driving. They are often to be seen in hand in the show ring.

These muscular horses have great presence and beauty. The neck is heavy, with a well-developed crest. The mane is abundant and should be kept long. The head-carriage is noble and high, the

Two Andalusians, named Domero and Blanco, played the part of Gandalf's mount, Shadowfax, in Lord of the Rings. *The part of Asfaloth was played by another Andalusian called Florian.*

forehead wide with expressive, medium-length ears. The eyes are dark-brown and gentle, the nostrils are flared, and the jaw is large and well-muscled. The withers are well-rounded and the shoulder is long and sloping. The chest is broad, the croup rounded, and the low-set tail is thick and long. The body is rounded and short-coupled, adding to the overall strength. The legs are strong with large joints and the hooves are rounded and compact.

The Andalusian is famous for its extravagant paces. Movement is elevated and extended, making the horse look as if it were floating on air. All paces are smooth, showy and spectacular.

Andalusians are proud and courageous, and although spirited to ride, they have amiable temperaments. They have soft mouths, making them extremely obedient when ridden properly.

Gray and bay coats are most in evidence, but others are accepted by the Andalusian Horse Association. In Spain, according to the studbook, only gray, bay and black are acceptable. Height is between 15 and 16.2hh.

ANGLO-ARAB

The Anglo-Arab derives its name from two of the world's greatest breeds, the Thoroughbred, which is of English (Anglo) origin, and the Arab. The rules of Anglo-Arab breeding in the United Kingdom are very strict, and only these two bloodlines can be present. Other countries have their own rules, with some adding elements of their own native breeds, the French Anglo-Arab being such a one. There are other stipulations, however, and at least 25 per cent Arab content is the norm.

Because the Anglo-Arab is a mixture of two breeds it is not actually recognized as such, with one exception: the fore-mentioned French Anglo-Arab. There are other variations which appear all over Europe, the Gidrán or Hungarian Anglo-Arab, the Shagya Arab, also from Hungary, the Russian Strelets-Arab, and Spain's Hispano-Arab.

Anglo-Arabs make superb riding horses and excel in most disciplines, including showjumping, eventing and dressage. They also do well in riding-horse showing classes, where, unlike the pure Arab, which must be left as it is, their manes and tails can be plaited. The combination of the Thoroughbred's complaisant nature and the strength, stamina and intelligence of the Arab make an ideal combination.

The interesting thing about breeding Anglo-Arabs is that one never know how they are going to turn out: they can be either predominantly Arab or Thoroughbred, or a combination of both; either way they are ideal all-rounders and extremely rewarding to ride.

The exciting blend of Thoroughbred and Arab combines the superior speed of the Thoroughbred with the better temperament of the Arabian.

The wind of heaven is that which blows
between a horse's ears.

Arabian Proverb

The Anglo-Arab should have the skeletal structure and conformation of a Thoroughbred and the tail and head-carriage of the Arab, though this can occasionally vary, with some having lighter bones than others. The head should have unmistakable Arab features, with a dished or straight profile that is not quite as extreme as the Arab's. The eyes should indicate that it can be spirited on occasions, while the nostrils are large and flared. The ears are medium-sized, fine, pointed and expressive. The head-carriage is fairly high, with a well-developed crest. The Anglo-Arab should have the good sloping shoulders, deep chest, and powerful hindquarters of the Thoroughbred. The tail-carriage can be either high like the Arab's or lower as in the Thoroughbred.

Anglo-Arabs are usually affectionate and intelligent. They are also brave and spirited and will always give of their very best. The most usual colors are brown, bay, chestnut and gray, while black is rather more rare. There is often white on the face and legs, but never on the rest of the body. Anglo-Arabs stand somewhere between 14.2 and 16.1hh.

The Anglo-Arab is popular in Europe and they are selectively bred in France and Poland, where they are almost exclusively used as sporthorses. The Anglo-Arab has also been instrumental in the development of the famous Selle Français showjumpers.

BASHKIR CURLY

The Bashkir was once bred by the Bashkiri people, living in the southern Urals. They used the horses to pull their troikas, while the mares' milk was used to make *kumiss,* a fermented alcoholic drink. The breed is very old and has evolved in an extraordinary fashion. It has the stocky body, large head and small nostrils common to horses raised in cold climates; but the strangest feature is its winter coat, which grows to a length of 6 inches, falling into tight ringlets.

The Bashkir is known in the United States as the Bashkir Curly. Some have also been imported into the United Kingdom, where they are used mainly for showing and

endurance riding. Back in their native land, however, they are used in harness and their long hair is spun into fabric; moreover, they are used for meat and their milk is still used. The Bashkir's blood is another strange factor, in that its composition is different from that of other horses; they also have higher respiratory and heart rates.

The original Bashkir had a large head with small ears. The eyes have an intelligent expression, the nose is straight, and the nostrils are small. The U.S. version has

The Bashkir has the wide-set eyes characteristic of Oriental breeds. This is said to give them a wider range of vision.

been bred with a smaller head, which appears to balance more neatly on the body. It has a well-developed neck, longish body, and the short stocky legs typical of horses from cold climates, where they develop a layer of fat in winter to keep themselves warm. Oddly enough, they shed out the mane hair (and sometimes even the tail) each summer, which grows back during winter. Foals arrive with thick, crinkly coats, curls inside their ears, and curly eyelashes.

Good-natured, affectionate and willing workers, Bashkirs are commonly chestnut, palomino or bay, and stand at about 14hh.

BELGIAN WARMBLOOD

This is a relatively new breed, having been carefully developed over several decades. It is the product of selective breeding, using Belgium's finest cavalry horses, as well as heavier breeds used in agriculture. The breed has also been improved with Thoroughbreds and Anglo-Arabs as well as with other already established European warmbloods, such as Hanoverian, Holstein, Selle Français and Dutch Warmblood. The result is a quality riding and competition horse excelling in international competition, particularly showjumping, eventing and dressage.

The Belgian Warmblood is near-perfect in conformation and has many of the Thoroughbred's characteristics. The head is of medium size with a straight nose and kind, alert eyes, while the neck forms a graceful arch and is long and well-developed. The chest is substantial with a deep girth and sloping shoulder. The back is of medium length with muscular loins

To ride a horse is to ride the sky.

Anon.

Belgian Warmbloods entered the American show scene in the 1970s, and the North American branch of the Belgian Warmblood Association was established in 1987.

and powerful quarters. The legs are strong, with large joints, and the hooves are well-shaped.

Belgian Warmbloods are much admired for their fluid paces, supple action, and jumping ability. They are spirited and courageous as well as kind and willing. Their height never deviates from between 16.1 and 16.2hh.

BRABANT

The Brabant, or Belgian Heavy Draft Horse, comes from the area of Belgium that has Brussels as its capital. It is of ancient origin, only slightly more recent than the Ardennais, to which it owes part of its lineage: the other part of its inheritance is thought to have stemmed from the Flanders Horse of the 11th to 16th centuries, which in turn is believed to have been descended from the ancient horses of the Quaternary period. For centuries Belgian breeders produced their stock by selective breeding, which also included inbreeding.

The Brabant's very existence is a direct result of the geology of the area: the rich heavy soil required a horse with great pulling power and big strong joints to enable it to lift its huge feet out of the thick clods of mud. As a result, three distinct bloodlines emerged 100 years ago, which intermingled to create the modern Brabant, These are the Gros de la Dendre, which is muscular and strong with huge legs; the Gris de Nivelles, with good conformation and a certain elegance; and the Colosse de la Mehaigne, which is large and has a lively temperament.

Over the centuries, the Brabant has had an enormous influence on today's modern breeds, much in the same way as the Arab bloodline has been added to improve existing stock. In the Middle Ages the horse was imported all over Europe and its bloodlines are also present in Germany's warmbloods. The Russians introduced native breeds to it to produce working horses and its influence is also present in the Shire, Irish Draft and Clydesdale, to name but a few. Today, Brabants are still part of the

The Brabant retains its pleasing conformation, despite being large. It has greatly contributed to the development of many of today's heavy breeds.

foundation stock for the breeding of warmbloods. They now appear throughout the world, where they are still used in agricultural work, logging and as dray horses. They also feature in the show ring.

The head is fairly square, with a straight profile, small pricked ears, and deep-set eyes with a kindly expression. The neck is short and very strong and set high with a large crest. The shoulders are sloping and the chest is wide and deep. The body is short, with a well-muscled back and strong quarters. The legs are fairly long and muscular and the hooves are large, rounded and tough; not much feathering is present.

The Brabant is so extremely docile as to be described as almost sluggish. But it is willing and obedient, and its pulling power is equal only to that of the Shire, for which it is highly prized. It is a hard worker with plenty of stamina and a strong constitution, and requires relatively little food for its size. Brabants are usually light chestnut with a flaxen mane; also acceptable is red roan, bay, dun and gray. It is a large animal and stands somewhere between 16.1 and 17hh.

CAMARGUE

The salt marshes and lagoons of the Rhône delta in south-eastern France are home to a race of semi-wild horses, that spend their time grazing on the sparse vegetation. This is a very ancient breed, that bears a striking resemblance to the primitive horses painted on cave-walls at Lascaux in prehistoric times. The Camargue's qualities were appreciated by Roman invaders on their way to the Iberian Peninsula, with the result that connexions were inevitably made with Spanish breeds.

The breed was further enhanced in the 19th century by infusions of Postier Breton, Arab, Thoroughbred, and Anglo-Arab bloodlines, though they seem to have had little bearing on the horses' overall appearance.

There is a round-up in the Camargue every year, when suitable horses are selected for riding purposes and substandard

animals are culled: this may seem ruthless but there is no doubt that it has led to improvements in the breed.

Camargue horses are traditionally ridden by the *gardiens* (Camargue cowboys), who use them for herding the famous black bulls of the region and for festivals in which their dazzling feats of horsemanship are displayed. The horses are also used for trekking the region, now a popular tourist attraction.

The head of the Camargue is rather square, with a broad forehead, short, broad ears, and expressive eyes. The neck is short and well-developed, the shoulder upright, and the back is short with a low-set tail. The legs are strong and the hooves well-

shaped and tough. The mane and tail are particularly abundant.

Camargues make obedient riding horses; they are extremely agile and have the ability to turn sharply at full gallop. As trekking ponies they are sure-footed and have plenty of stamina. However, they never quite lose their independent spirit and something of their wild inheritance is always retained. They are invariably gray, though other colors sometimes appear. Foals are born dark but become gray as they mature. They are from 13.1–14.2hh.

To visit the Camargue would be unthinkable without seeing the famous 'white' horses, that have been there for centuries.

CLEVELAND BAY

The excellent Cleveland Bay is Britain's oldest breed and originated in medieval times. Gradually, however, it became rarer, and numbers dipped to a critical level in the last century. Thankfully, it is gaining in popularity once more, and numbers have begun to increase.

The breed is related to the Chapman Horse, which lived in north-east Yorkshire in the Middle Ages and which received Iberian and Barb bloodlines. Clevelands were then mainly used as packhorses and for agricultural work, when they were greatly admired for their strength and ability to carry heavy loads for long distances. The name comes from the area (Cleveland) where they were bred and the fact that their color is bay. Later on, the breed was crossed with Thoroughbred to produce a lighter, elegant carriage horse, which is a feature of the Cleveland Bay today. Sadly, the previous type has become extinct.

The Cleveland Bay was very popular in times past, but the development of motorized transport heralded its demise and the breed had been reduced to an all-time low by the 1970s. In some respects, however, they are still very much in

There is something about the outside of a horse that is good for the inside of a man.

Winston Churchill

evidence; Cleveland Bays have been kept at the royal mews since King George V first introduced them, and the Hampton Court Stud still actively breeds them for state and ceremonial occasions.

Today, Cleveland Bays and part-breds can be seen in showjumping, dressage, eventing, driving and hunting, where they are admired for their sure-footedness and great stamina.

The horse possesses a large noble head on a long muscular neck, which is attached to a sloping shoulder and a long, deep body. The strong, shortish legs have plenty of bone and no feathers.

Clevelands are calm and intelligent and are seemingly able to think for themselves. They are honest, strong and confident, with enormous powers of endurance that have become legendary.

They are exclusively bays, with a rich black mane and tail and black-stockinged legs with no traces of white. They stand between 16 and 17hh.

Her Majesty Queen Elizabeth II is patron of the Cleveland Bay Horse Society, dedicated to preserving the breed, which it describes as a British horse with a history and a future.

CLYDESDALE

The establishment of the Scottish Clydesdale began in the late-17th century when Lanarkshire farmers and various dukes of Hamilton supposedly imported Flemish stallions, ancestors of the Brabant, to Scotland. The farmers were skillful breeders and mated them with native heavy draft mares already in existence; over the next 100 years or so, English Shire, Friesian and Cleveland Bay blood was also added. The result was known as the Clydesdale and it was highly prized as a draft horse. The Clydesdale Horse Society was established in 1877, almost a century and a half after the breed first began to evolve.

The breed soon became popular as a general farm horse and also for hauling loads over long and short distances; Clydesdales could be found in most major

cities of Scotland, the North of England and Northern Ireland, as well as in agricultural areas. In fact, the horse became popular the world over, when considerable numbers were imported to North America, Canada and Australia.

Clydesdales are very different from the usual heavy draft horses, which tend to be plain-looking and squat; in fact, it looks positively refined, having a short-coupled body, long legs, and a high head-carriage. As with all heavy horses, the Clydesdale

A PORTRAIT OF THE HORSE

The outstanding characteristics of this famous horse are a combination of weight, size and activity, but what is particularly admired is the exceptional durability of the Clydesdale's feet and limbs. They are surprisingly agile for their size.

breed began to decline with the development of motorized transport and reached an even lower ebb in the 1960s and '70s. A few families kept the breed going, however, and today numbers are rising. Nevertheless, the Clydesdale continues to be classified as 'at risk' by the Rare Breeds Society. Today they are highly valued in the show ring as well as in harness; as dray horses, they often take part in displays, and are even used to pull wedding carriages.

The head is proudly held, and the medium, well-shaped ears are pricked and alert; the eyes are kind and intelligent. It has a slightly Roman nose and the nostrils are large. The neck is long and well-set, with a high crest leading to high withers. The back is slightly concave and short and the quarters are well-developed and powerful. The legs are straight and long with plenty of feathering. The feet are large and require careful shoeing if contracted heels are not to develop.

These charming horses are energetic with an alert, cheerful air. They are even-tempered and enjoy company. They are extremely strong with a lively action and a slight tendency to dish.

Clydesdales can be bay, brown and black and usually have white patches all the way up the legs and under the belly, which can turn roan in places. They are usually around 16.2hh, but some males may reach 17hh or more.

CONNEMARA

The Connemara is Ireland's only native breed, although it is not indigenous to the country. It is thought that it was brought to Ireland 2,500 years ago when the Celts settled in Ireland and brought their ponies with them. The Celts were traders and traveled to and from Mediterranean ports, which makes it likely that their ponies were of Oriental descent, probably Barb. In medieval times these horses were bred with the Irish Hobeye, which was a much coveted riding horse, famous for its speed, agility and endurance.

Legend has it that further blood was added to the breed when the Spanish Armada sunk off the coast of Ireland and Iberian horses swam ashore and mated with native breeds. Later on, the breed was further improved with infusions of Hackney, Welsh Cob, Irish Draft, Clydesdale and Thoroughbred bloodlines.

The Connemara derives its name from the region of that name, which included Connaught and Galway a few hundred years ago. The terrain is rocky and mountainous with very little vegetation. The weather can be atrocious with piercing winds and driving rain coming in from the Atlantic. Consequently, the Connemara has evolved into an extremely hardy specimen, which is sure-footed and agile and has extraordinary jumping abilities.

Historically, it was used as a draft animal, transporting peat and seaweed as well as taking potatoes and corn to market. Nowadays it is used for hunting, eventing, showjumping and driving; it is often crossed with the Thoroughbred to produce an excellent jumping horse.

Semi-wild Connemara ponies can still be seen, peacefully grazing in their native rugged terrain.

The Connemara is a riding pony of excellent quality. The head is fine and set quite high, with small pricked ears, clever eyes, and a straight nose with fairly large nostrils. The neck is of medium length and well-muscled and the shoulders are sloping; it has a deep girth, a straight back, and well-developed quarters. The legs are short, but elegant and strong, with very hard hooves. Intelligent animals, they have a calm and kindly disposition. They are excellent all-rounders and being hardy are easy to maintain. They are most commonly gray, but also bay, black, dun and brown. They stand between 13 and 14.2hh.

DANISH WARMBLOOD

The story of the Danish Warmblood begins in Holstein, which until the mid-19th century was Danish territory and allowed the Danes easy access to German warmblood stock through the Cistercian monasteries of Holstein. For centuries the monks had been breeding the old-style heavy Holstein with highly-bred Iberian stallions to produce useful multi-purpose horses; these practices were therefore far from new.

The Royal Frederiksborg Stud, which was founded in 1562 near Copenhagen, was already breeding Andalusians and Neapolitans, and this stock was interbred with a small Danish breed and the larger Jutland Heavy Draft (both coldbloods), with infusions of Turkish and Dutch breeds and later English Thoroughbred added. This created the excellent all-rounder, known as the Frederiksborg, for which the monks of Holstein had been striving. The stud closed in 1862, but some of the stock survived in the hands of private breeders.

By the middle of the 20th century, the Danes realized that they needed to create a competition sporthorse of superb quality to rival other European breeds. Subsequently, they decided to breed the Frederiksborg-Thoroughbred mares with Thoroughbred, Anglo-Norman, Trakehner, Wielkopolski and Malopolski stallions to create the truly superb Danish Warmblood. It is interesting to note that Hanoverian was not used, which is unusual, as the bloodline is present in most other European warmblood breeds.

Danish Warmbloods are the supreme masters of high-level competition, though the less talented still make wonderful all-purpose riding horses. They particularly excel at dressage and showjumping.

Dansk Varmblod holds a Young Horses Championship every year, designed to assess the caliber of the five-year-old offspring of the stock of Danish Warmblood stallions and brood mares. Tests are rigorous and include dressage and showjumping.

The conformation of the Danish Warmblood is near-perfect: it has a noble head with large, intelligent eyes and fairly long, tapered ears. All elements of the body are in perfect proportion, from the long, well-developed neck to the straight well-boned legs and shapely feet. It is admired for its fluid paces and supple action, which makes it so popular as a dressage horse. It is spirited and courageous but at the same time kind and willing. It is most commonly bay, but all solid colors are acceptable. A little white is permitted on the head and legs. It stands usually around 16.2hh.

DARTMOOR

There is evidence to suggest that ponies inhabited Dartmoor as early as 2000 BC, a fact confirmed by remains excavated on Shaugh Moor. The earliest written reference to the Dartmoor is in the will of Awifold of Crediton, who died in 1012. The breed stems from the Celtic Pony, which went on to breed with other British natives; later, there were additions of Roadster, Welsh Pony, Cob, Arab, and in recent times, Thoroughbred.

The Dartmoor pony comes from the county of Devon in the south-west of England and gets its name from the area of wild moorland which it still roams. Standing over 1,000ft (305m) above sea

In medieval times, Dartmoor Ponies were used to carry heavy loads of tin from the mines on Dartmoor; but when the mines were closed, they were allowed to roam free.

level, with wind and rain driving off the sea, it is at times an inhospitable place, with rocky outcrops and sparse vegetation. Consequently, the pony is extremely hardy and sure-footed and has plenty of stamina.

Dartmoors fail to thrive if left solely to their own devices, however, and require extra hay in winter, which farmers put out for them. This was confirmed during the Second World War, when Dartmoor was completely out of bounds. As a result, the population dwindled to only two stallions and 12 mares because of the lack of supplementary feeding. Nowadays the breed has been greatly improved and with careful monitoring is now flourishing. Children like to ride Dartmoors and they are also used for showing and driving.

The Dartmoor has a small, nicely-set neat head, with small, alert ears and an intelligent and kindly eye. The neck is of medium length and fairly well-developed, as are the back, loins and quarters. The tail is high-set, the legs are shapely but sturdy, and the hooves are well-formed and hard.

Dartmoors make excellent children's ponies, and their small size makes them easily manageable. They also have kind and docile natures.

The Dartmoor's most striking feature is that it moves with almost no knee flexion: this produces a long, free-flowing stride similar to that of a horse and is very comfortable for the rider. They are mainly bay and brown with only a little white on the legs and face. Height is up to 12.2hh.

If wishes were horses, beggars might ride

English Proverb

DØLE-GUDBRANDSDAL

The Døle-Gudbrandsdal originated in the Gudbrandsdal valley, which is situated between the city of Oslo in Norway and the North Sea coast. Though much bigger, they are not dissimilar to the Dales and Fell ponies of Great Britain and they are thought to share much of the same ancestry, namely the prehistoric Celtic Pony and the Friesian horse. This is feasible as the Friesian people are reputed to have traded all over Europe as well as in the British Isles and Scandinavia.

The Døle was crossed with other breeds over the centuries, such as Heavy Draft, Norfolk Trotter, Arab and Thoroughbred. The result was a horse that was strong and heavy enough for both haulage and riding.

Today there is another Døle type, created when the original horse was extensively bred with Thoroughbreds to produce the Døle Trotter, which is still used for trotting races in Norway.

The Døle is one of the smallest of the coldbloods, with an excellent trot and great pulling power. The Thoroughbred stallion Odin, imported in 1834, is said to have had a particularly lasting influence on the breed.

The Second World War saw a depletion in numbers, but since 1962 efforts have been made to improve the quality of the horses; the breed society will only register stallions with sound conformation and a good race-track record. Døle's are still used on farms and are particularly useful in agricultural and forestry work.

The Døle is the smallest of the draft horses and resembles a large pony. The head is small and neat with a broad forehead, straight or slightly Roman nose, and a square muzzle. The ears are small and alert and the eyes kind but inquisitive. The neck is short and well-developed, with a slight crest. The chest and shoulders are very strong, the girth is deep, and the back is long with powerful, well-muscled hindquarters. The legs are short, with good bone and feathering around the heels, and the hooves are hard.

The Døle is a hardy breed, well able to withstand harsh winter conditions. It requires a modicum of care but can survive on little food. It is even-tempered and a willing worker. Usually bay, brown, chestnut or black, they can occasionally be gray or dun. The Trotter types often have white on their legs and faces. They stand between 14.2 and 15.1hh.

107

DON

The Don is Russia's most famous breed. It originated in the harsh Russian steppes, where it once roamed in herds, surviving the freezing winters and torrid summers with nothing but sparse vegetation for food.

The original steppes breed, known as the Old Don, was bred with various Orientals, such as the Arab, Karabakh and Turkmene, and Orlov and Thoroughbred were added to improve its conformation and provide it with incredible stamina.

The horse was the preferred mount of the Don Cossacks; it was also used by the Russian army, and its extreme toughness made it an excellent hunter, particularly of wolves. Today, the Don's hardy constitution makes it an excellent endurance horse. It is also used to improve other breeds.

The overall picture of the Don is one of strength and robustness. The head is fairly small and neat, the slightly dished or straight nose clearly indicating its Arab heritage. Ears are small and shapely and the eyes are large and intelligent. The neck is set high and should be arched; however, many have ewe necks. The back is fairly long, straight and wide, with sloping quarters and a straight shoulder. The legs are clean but in some cases can be sickle-hocked. Moreover, the placement of the pelvis tends to restrict movement and causes a stilted action – a fault that has now been largely bred out. The hooves are well-shaped and hard.

Tough and sturdy, with an independent spirit, these qualities have found their way into other breeds. The most striking feature of the Don's coat is its iridescent sheen. It is most commonly chestnut, but can also be bay, brown, black and gray. It stands approximately 15.2hh.

DUTCH WARMBLOOD

The Dutch Warmblood is a relatively new breed, its stud book having been opened in the Netherlands in 1958. It is now enjoying huge success in showjumping and dressage and is in demand worldwide as a top-class competition horse.

The Dutch Warmblood differs from most European warmbloods, in that it was not based on a breed which existed in a slightly different form in previous centuries, and which has been improved. It contains

No hour of life is wasted that is spent in the saddle.

Winston Churchill

breeds from all over Europe. The Dutch Warmblood was evolved from the Gelderlander and the heavier Groningen, which have been in existence in the Netherlands since the Middle Ages. The breeds themselves consist of many European strains, the Gelderlander being a combination of Andalusian, Norman,

Oldenburg, Hackney and Thoroughbred strains, to name but a few. The Groningen was created from Friesian and Oldenburg stock, which was chosen to produce good paces, correct conformation, and a strong presence. A kind and willing nature and a certain amount of hardiness were also considered to be valuable traits.

Initially, the Dutch Warmblood was created by mating Gelderlander and Groningen, and Thoroughbred was added later to correct remaining conformation faults. The result was a little temperamental

in character, and to improve this, Hanoverian and Selle Français were added for level-headedness and acquiescence.

The Dutch Warmblood is lighter than many warmbloods. The head is attractive, with an intelligence and alertness reflected in the large, lively eyes and medium-sized

The most internationally important Dutch Warmblood type is the Riding Horse Type (Rijpaardtype), a distinctly modern, elegant sporthorse bred for athleticism, good character, and soundness.

The Show Driving Type (Tuigpaardtype) is an extravagant, stylish, high-stepping carriage horse – shown rather like the American Saddlebred fine harness horse.

pricked ears. The neck is well-set, long and muscular. The withers are prominent and the back is short and straight, with powerful, slightly sloping quarters and a high-set tail. The shoulders are sloping and the legs are long and well-developed, with strong, shapely hooves.

What makes this horse such a competent performer at dressage and showjumping is its extravagant and elastic paces. It also has a sensible attitude to work, with the added spark needed to perform each action superlatively well. It is also equable and amenable, and its flowing action means that it is comfortable to ride.

Dutch Warmbloods are most commonly bay, chestnut or gray. Black and coloreds are also possible. They stand at 16hh and over.

EXMOOR

The Exmoor is truly ancient, said to have existed before the last Ice Age, when similar ponies migrated south from Alaska, and where bones matching those of the modern pony have been found. Exmoor's isolated position, covering remote areas of the counties of Devon and Somerset in England, has ensured that very little cross-breeding has occurred, which has maintained the purity of the breed; indeed, the Exmoor pony is one of the purest breeds in the world, unlike its near cousin, the Dartmoor, which having been more accessible to other influences, has been subjected to more evolutions.

Exmoors are truly wild ponies and they still live up on the moors. Being regarded as

The Exmoor is a rare and unique survivor. It has existed on the moor with little human interference, except for the annual 'harvest' of young animals.

a rare breed, with only 1,000 ponies worldwide, they are now closely monitored. There are aproximately 300 breeding mares in the U.K., producing around 130 foals a year. Half of these mares still live on Exmoor and to protect the purity of the breed each foal is inspected, numbered and branded with the society's mark on the flank and the herd number on the shoulder.

Various farms in the area are involved in the breeding of the Exmoor ponies, with the result that their future is now much brighter. Nowadays, Exmoors are also being bred in other parts of Britain, but the moors ponies

are still used as foundation stock to ensure the purity of the breed.

The Exmoor's head is large, with a broad forehead and hooded eyes (known as 'toad-eyes') to protect them from the elements. The ears are thick and short and the nose is straight. The neck is also thick and well-developed, with a deep chest; the short, fine legs are nevertheless muscular, with a little feathering around the fetlocks. The hooves are small and hard. The coat is dense with a thick, wiry mane and tail.

Exmoors are extremely tough and can live out all-year-round. If they are to be domesticated, they must be caught and broken in while young. They are good-natured, willing and obedient and make good children's ponies.

Exmoors can be bay, brown or dun with black points. There should be no white, but the distinctive mealy markings should be present around the eyes, muzzle and flanks. Mares should not exceed 12.2hh or stallions 12.3hh.

FELL

The Fell is closely related to the Dales Pony, though it originated on the western side of the Pennines, inhabiting the hills and mountains of Cumbria in north-eastern England. It is a descendant of the Celtic Pony, that once roamed much of northern Europe, and which the Romans used as draft animals and in raids against the Picts. They were later used by reivers – the cattle-raiders of the Scottish Border country – because they were known to be sure-footed and with plenty of stamina.

Vikings used the ponies for plowing and sled-pulling, the Normans for shepherding, and by the 13th century, Fells were hauling goods in Belgium's thriving wool industry.

The Fell's checkered history became more eventful, when they were used by smugglers around Britain's northern coast. They were also bred by Cistercian monks, who introduced gray ponies to signify that they belonged to the monastery.

Over the years, and like the Dales, the breed was improved by mating with other stock, such as the Friesian, to which the Fell bears a resemblance. However, it remains much purer then the Dales, which has been subjected to rather more added bloodstock.

Like many native breeds, numbers declined during and after the two world wars, when farms switched to machinery and motorized transport as they became more readily available. The Fell, however, remained popular as a riding and driving pony and its fortunes have been happily reversed. Today the Fell is an all-round family pony, strong enough to carry an adult and docile enough for children to ride. They make excellent trekking ponies, making them popular with the tourist industry. They are also used in harness and are still used occasionally to herd sheep.

The Fell bears a strong resemblance to the Friesian. The head is noble, with a broad forehead and a straight or slightly dished, tapering nose, with large flaring nostrils. The eyes are proud and intelligent and the ears small and neat. The head sits well on the neck, which is of medium length, strong but not overdeveloped. The shoulders are well-muscled and sloping, ensuring a good smooth action. The body is sturdy with a strong back and deep chest. The legs are strong and muscular, with fine feathering present on the backs of the legs; the hooves are well-shaped and are the characteristic blue color. Mane and tail should not be trimmed but should be left to grow naturally.

The Fell Pony has an excellent constitution and like most mountain and moorland ponies it is hardy and able to live out all-year-round. It is easy-going and enjoys the company of humans beings; however, it is a free spirit and can be willful on occasions. Fell Ponies are famous for their excellent paces, which make them comfortable to ride. They excel at endurance events and are fast into the bargain, which is an asset in harness.

Fells are usually pure black with no white markings, but bay, gray and brown are also possible. A small amount of white is permissable around the fetlocks or in the form of a small star on the forehead. They stand around 14hh.

Because the Fell Pony runs very true to type, it is that much easier to find matched pairs for driving.

FJORD

The Norwegian Fjord is most likely descended from the Przewalski or Asiatic Wild Horse, which in turn was descended from Ice Age horses. It seems to have retained many of its ancestors' characteristics, including the pale coat, the dorsal stripe down the back, and the occasional zebra stripes on the legs, which were typical of the ancient breed.

The primitive breed was improved over many hundreds of years by breeding with the Celtic Pony and Tarpan. The result has been used for thousands of years, and there is evidence of its use in raids and battles from Viking artifacts. The Vikings had a particularly bloodthirsty approach to selection: they allowed stallions to fight to the death, ensuring that the stronger specimens continued the breed.

Fjords still have their manes clipped in the manner seen on Viking rune stones; the mane is unusual in that the hair is cream on the outer edges and black in the center, being a part of the dorsal stripe. The mane is therefore clipped so that the black part remains prominent.

The Fjord has been used to improve many other Northern European breeds, including the Icelandic and Highland. Today it can be seen over most of Scandinavia, mainly as children's riding ponies. It is sure-footed and excellent at trekking and long-distance endurance events. It is also popular in harness, where it has been successful in competition. Some are still used around the farm for light plowing and as packhorses.

The Fjord has an attractive head: it is short and wide with short, neat ears, a slightly dished face and large nostrils. The

All breeding in Norway is now under government control, and only champion stock can be exported. Fjords now have registries in the U.S., Canada and elsewhere. Twenty-two Fjords have been imported to the U.S., most of them in the 1950s.

eyes are large and kind, and the neck is short and thick, accentuated by the traditionally clipped mane. The body is sturdy, with sloping quarters and a low-set tail. The legs are strong with plenty of bone and the feet are tough and hard.

Fjords are usually a pale gold or dun color, with a black dorsal stripe running from the poll to the tail; this also runs through the center of the mane, giving the horses their primitive appearance, the outer sections of which are white. Some also have zebra stripes on the legs. They stand between 13.2 and 14.2hh.

FRENCH TROTTER

The first race track used for trotting in France opened in Cherbourg in 1839, and the sport has never looked back since then. The first races were a means of selecting suitable stallions and became quite an event. The most popular trotters at that time were Norman and Anglo-Norman breeds; later, these were crossed with Norfolk Roadsters from Britain, and by the end of the 19th century the breed had been further enhanced by infusions of British Hackney, Orlov Trotter from Russia, and Thoroughbred. These breeds did much to create a popular and much respected trotter, and a later addition of American Standardbred seems to have completed the breed.

In 1906 a stud book was created for French Trotters, though the breed itself wasn't recognized as such until 1922. To be acceptable for registration it was necessary that the horse be able to trot .62 mile (1 km) in 1 minute 42 seconds. This was later extended to include only horses whose parents had both been registered, thus ensuring the purity of the breed. Recently, however, even more infusions of Standardbred have been made to improve the breed and its paces; the result is a world-class trotting horse, said to be able to surpass the Standardbred itself.

Today the French Trotter is predominantly used for the sport for which it was bred, both under saddle and in harness; however, they also make good riding horses and even jumpers. The horses that have been bred for riding have also been used to sire competition horses – the Selle Français in particular.

In appearance, the French Trotter's Thoroughbred ancestry is much in evidence in the noble head, broad forehead, medium-sized far-apart ears, and kind, intelligent eyes. The nostrils are large and flaring. The neck is long and well-developed, with a straight shoulder, deep chest, and well-formed, powerful quarters. The legs are muscular with plenty of bone and well-shaped hooves.

The French Trotter has all the fine characteristics of the Thoroughbred. It has a good turn of speed, plenty of stamina, and a kind and even temperament, though it is not without spirit. The harness horses are usually a little smaller and lighter than the ridden types. Like the Thoroughbred, all solid colors can be seen, with the occasional roan. Grays are quite rare. Trotters stand at around 16.2hh.

Mostly bred in Normandy, most French breeders have no more than two or three mares and they often breed, school, train and race their horses themselves.

FRIESIAN

The Friesian is the Netherlands' only surviving indigenous breed. It is descended from a native breed that once roamed Friesland – the western part of the ancient region of Frisia – 3,000 years ago, and where the remains of a similar coldblooded horse have been found. As riding horses, the Friesian's history is an ancient one, with evidence that it was used by Roman soldiers when they were building Hadrian's Wall in around AD 150; this is

You will hear the beat of a horse's feet,
And the swish of a skirt in the dew,
Steadily cantering through
The misty solitudes,
As though they perfectly knew
The old lost road through the woods…

Rudyard Kipling

supported by the fact that Fell and Dales breeds, native to the English Pennines, are also descended from Friesian stock. Friesian bloodlines are also present in the Orlov Trotter and in most American trotters.

Over the years, the original, rather heavy and plain breed was infused with Oriental and Andalusian blood; this improved the breed to such an extent that during the 17th century, Friesians could be seen performing *haute école* alongside Spanish horses, and Friesians were in demand as elegant

A feature of the Friesian horse is its long mane and tail. When showing, these are not cut and the tail often reaches the ground.

carriage horses. During the 19th century, however, the Friesian became something of a rarity, being almost exclusively restricted to Friesland, where it was used as a general riding horse and trotter. By the end of the First World War, the Friesian was in dire peril of extinction, with only three stallions and a few mares still in existence. Fortunately, with careful breeding and an infusion of Oldenburg blood, the Friesian is once again flourishing; today, it is in evidence all over the world – admired for its noble presence and expressive trot, which is particularly striking in harness. It is still used in *haute école* disciplines.

The head is proud and of medium size, with small, alert ears pointing slightly inward. The eyes are kindly and expressive, the head-carriage is high and elegant, and the neck is of medium length with a high

The Friesian was traditionally used in farming and to draw Friesian gigs. It is also found in circuses and is used in driving contests.

crest. The withers are well-developed, tapering into the back muscles, and the shoulders sloping. The back is of medium length, strong and straight, leading to well-developed loins and quarters. The legs are clean and strong with slight feathering, and the mane and tail are long and luxuriant; when showing, mane and tail should be left untrimmed. The Friesian has a proud bearing and is gentle and amenable if rather energetic. It is always black, and only the smallest of stars is permitted on the forehead. Usually Friesians stand around 15–15.2hh, but some Friesians have been bred larger, reaching more than 16hh.

FURIOSO

As a breed, the Hungarian Furioso has existed for only about 150 years. It was developed by Hungary's famous Mezöhegyes Stud, which was founded by the Habsburg Emperor Joseph II in 1785; it is also where the Nonius was bred.

In 1840 the stud imported an English Thoroughbred called Furioso, and in 1843 another, North Star, which was a Norfolk Roadster. They mated these two with Nonius and Arab mares, the result being two very distinctive breeds, the Furioso and the North Star. By 1885, however, the two breeds had merged to such an extent that only one breed remained, with Furioso traits predominating.

Today the Furioso is used as an all-round riding horse and excellent jumper, and its remarkable stamina makes it a highly competent steeplechaser.

The Furioso is a quality horse, and possesses all the attributes of its Thoroughbred forebears. The head is fine, with a straight nose leading to a squarish muzzle. The ears are medium-length and shapely, and the eyes are inquisitive and bold. The neck is long and elegant, with fine sloping shoulders; the girth is deep and the legs are long and strong. The quarters are well-developed with a high tail-carriage.

Most noticeable is the action of the high-stepping knee, which is inherited from the Nonius. The Furioso makes an elegant carriage horse as well as a riding horse; it has the amenability of the Thoroughbred, together with its spirit and courage.

Furiosos are usually brown, black or bay, with only the minimum of white markings. They stand at around 16.1hh.

During the Second World War, the Mezöhegyes-bred Furiosos were destroyed, only to be renewed from stock discovered in the Hungarian countryside. Besides Hungary and Rumania, Furiosos are also bred in Bulgaria and the former Yugoslavia.

GELDERLANDER

The Gelderlander, or Gelderland, is a warmblood that originated in the province of Gelder in the Netherlands. The breed was originally created by Dutch farmers, who required an all-round

workhorse for their own use, as well as an animal they could sell on as a good-quality riding and carriage horse.

Native heavy mares from the Gelder were bred with Andalusian, Neapolitan, Norman, Norfolk Roadster and Holstein stallions to produce a well-built horse. In

Years of careful breeding has resulted in the Gelderlander – a horse with very special qualities. The breed may have been the product of other bloodlines, but more important was the removal of unwanted characteristics by rigorous methods of selection.

the 19th century the breed was further improved when East Friesian, Oldenburg, Hackney and Thoroughbred were introduced.

When mechanization made the farmhorse redundant in the 1960s and '70s, it was consciously decided to transform the Gelderland into a lighter riding horse. Today it is an excellent all-rounder, with a talent for showjumping, its high-stepping action having presumably been inherited from its trotter forebears.

The Gelderland appears in the ancestry of other modern warmbloods, notably the Dutch Warmblood, which was established as a breed in the late 1950s. There are very few Gelderlanders in existence, now that the Dutch Warmblood has overtaken them in popularity. However, there are a few interested persons who strive to keep the old breed alive.

Gelderlanders have a plain but well-porportioned head, with a straight or slightly Roman nose. The ears are fine, shapely and expressive, and the eyes are kind. The neck is fairly long and muscular, with a slightly pronounced crest. The withers are prominent and the back is long and straight, with a short croup and high-set tail. The girth is deep with a long, sloping shoulder, strong, muscular legs and large, tough hooves.

The Gelderlander has a charming, easy-going disposition and is a willing worker. They are usually chestnut, although black, bay and gray are often seen. There is a good deal of white on the head and legs. They stand around 15.2–16.2hh.

...I heard a neigh. Oh, such a brisk and melodious neigh as that was! My very heart leaped with delight at the sound.

Nathaniel Hawthorne

GIARA

The Giara, a hardy and agile pony, lives wild in the middle of Sardinia on the Altopiano della Giara plateau, nearly 2,000ft above sea level and an hour's drive from the town of Oristano.

The Giara dates back to the Bronze Age, when it could be found all over Sardinia. A few of them were domesticated, and the rest roamed wild, finding a safe habitat on the plateau, where they had no natural enemies.

The severity of their environment has greatly influenced the character and

Show me your horse and I will show you what you are.

Anon.

conformation of these animals. Today, they live in small herds of 20 or so, made up of one stallion with mares, youngsters and foals. When the young stallions grow to maturity, they leave the herd and start a new group of their own.

In the wild, the Giara pony is shy, bad-tempered and wary of human beings, though domesticated lines can be ridden by children and make good sport ponies.

They have square heads with a large jaw. Their profile is compact, with a wide forehead, large, bright eyes, and small pointed ears. The neck is short, with a thick mane and a low wither. Shoulders are straight, strong and well-muscled, and the back is long, with the tail carried low. Legs are short and strong and the hooves are hard to cope with the rough conditions.

Colors are usually black or bay. Giaras stand at around 50 inches tall.

The plateau, where these famous wild ponies live, has recently been declared a UNESCO World Heritage Site.

GRONINGEN

The Groningen's bloodline has been of vital importance in the breeding of modern warmbloods in the Netherlands, the prototype being an old Dutch breed which originated in the north-eastern province of Groningen. It was bred for use as a heavyweight riding horse as well as for general farm use.

The breed was established by crossing East Friesian and German Oldenburg with the native stock of the area. A heavier horse was needed to farm the heavy soil of the region, so Suffolk Punch and Norfolk Roadster stallions were also introduced to make the Groningen a more substantial animal than its near neighbor, the Gelderlander, which came from a region that had lighter soil.

Both horses are the foundation of the now internationally famous Dutch Warmblood, and the powerful well-developed quarters of the Groningen can be clearly seen in the new breed, which is an excellent showjumper. Nowadays, however, the Groningen, along with the Gelderlander, is a rare breed.

The Groningen has a long, rather plain head with long ears and a docile expression. The neck is medium-length and well-developed, and the withers are prominent; the back is long, the croup flattened, and the tail is set high, with very muscular quarters. The girth is deep and the legs are short and strong with plenty of bone. The hooves are well-shaped.

Groningens are good-natured and amenable. They have great strength, stamina and power – attributes which it has passed on to the Dutch Warmblood. They are mainly black, brown or bay and stand around 15.3–16.1hh.

After 1945, the demand for versatility prompted breeders to produce a more compact animal, with greater freedom of movement. The old Groningen can hardly be said to exist today, and the breed as a whole is now something of a rarity.

GYPSY VANNER

The origins of the Gypsy Vanner, or Drummer Horse, lie with the Irish Travelers, or Gypsies, of the British Isles. The relationship between Gypsies and horses goes back hundreds of years, but it was only some 50 years ago that it came to be regarded as a special breed. Until recently, the Irish Cob or traditional colored cob was considered to be more of a type than a breed, until finally, in 1996, it was recognized and registered as a breed.

Crossed with Friesian, Shire, Dales Pony and Clydesdale, it is now a heavy horse, variable in size and appearance.

Gypsy Vanner is the American term for the Irish Cob or piebald horse, also known in parts of Europe as the Irish Tinker Horse, although 'tinker' is regarded as a derogatory word and is no longer used. The larger type, that can reach 16hh, is also known as the Drummer Horse, though its connections with the cavalry are tenuous to say the least.

The Gypsy Vanner's build is powerful and compact. It should have a 'sweet head', meaning that it is in proportion with the rest of the body. It has an abundant mane and plenty of feathering. The chest should be broad and the withers rounded; the knees should be large and flat and the hooves substantial.

Although known for its extreme docility, it is also intelligent and athletic; it must be sound enough, both mentally and physically, to endure a lifetime on the road. It comes in all colors, including piebald and skewbald, and stands between 14 and 15.2hh.

Gipsy gold does not chink and glitter.
It gleams in the sun and neighs in the dark.

Attributed to the Claddaugh Gypsies of Galway, Ireland

HACKNEY

The Hackney breed first emerged in the 18th and 19th centuries in Norfolk and Yorkshire, where it was used by farmers who prized it for its stamina. Later on, it came to be used for sport, particularly for trotting, both in harness and under saddle, and was capable of amazing speeds: one mare, Nonpareil, is said to have trotted 100 miles (160km) in just under ten hours. But it was as a high-stepping carriage horse that the Hackney was principally known: this made it indispensable until the 1920s, when it was gradually replaced by the automobile.

The English Hackney owes its trotting ability to its breeding: its probable foundation stock consisted of Norfolk and Yorkshire Trotter, which was bred with Thoroughbred and Arab for heightened performance. Hackney ponies are also derived from English Trotters, with additions of Fell and Welsh Pony. Hackney horses and ponies both have a registered stud book, which was opened in 1883.

Today the Hackney is underutilized, usually seen only in the show ring, where its extravagant paces are demonstrated, harnessed to smart renovated carriages. But they are beginning to be seen in driving competitions and even in dressage, eventing and showjumping. They are also mated with other breeds to produce enhancements of the modern sporthorse.

The Hackney's head-carriage is high and proud. It has fine, alert ears and intelligent eyes, while the nose is straight or slightly Roman. The neck is long and well-developed, with a high crest leading to good sloping shoulders and a short-coupled body.

The quarters are strong and powerful and the legs sturdy with plenty of bone.

Hackneys are lively, fiery animals and most definitely not for the novice. They have enormous stamina and the ability to trot for many miles without tiring. They are best known for their extravagant action, where the front legs are brought up very high, before being flung straight out from the shoulder.

They are mostly bay, brown and black, and chestnut and roan are sometimes seen. There is usually white on the head and face. Hackney ponies stand between 12 and 14hh, while the horses are around 14.2–15.2hh.

Sadly, the Hackney is now on the list of endangered species. There are only about 2,500 horses left in the world and approximately 150 of these are in the U.S.

HAFLINGER

The history of the Haflinger is obscure and there are various opinions as to its true origins. It is thought to have come from the South Tyrol in Austria, close to its border with Italy; borders have changed many times throughout history, however, making the exact location impossible to pinpoint. However, the Haflinger is not unlike the slightly larger Italian Avelignese, and they probably had common ancestors.

The Haflinger may have been the result of native stock breeding with Oriental horses, which were left behind when the Ostrogoths were driven north by the Byzantine forces in the 6th century AD. Another story is that King Louis IV of Germany gave a Burgundian stallion to his son as a wedding gift, which was mated with local mares of Oriental origin to produce the Haflinger breed; either way it would seem that Oriental bloodlines are present.

What is known for sure, however, is that the modern Haflinger breed was improved in 1868, when the Arab stallion, El-Bedavi XXII, was imported to the region and bred

No one can teach riding so well as a horse

C.S. Lewis

with Haflinger mares; today, all Haflingers are related to this one stallion.

Today the Haflinger is still to be found in Austria, where it is closely monitored, not only in government-organized breeding programs but also by private individuals. The breed is popular the world over, particularly in Europe, where it is used in the forests and farms of the Tyrol. It is also useful in harness, and as a children's riding pony and family pet.

The Arab influence can be clearly seen in the Haflinger's fine head, which presents a sharp contrast to the stocky body. The nose is slightly dished, and the eyes are large and attentive. The ears are small and alert and the nostrils and muzzle neat. The neck is well-proportioned, with fine sloping shoulders, good withers, and a deep girth. The body is broad and strong, with muscular quarters and a high-set tail. The legs are of medium length with strong, tough hooves.

The Haflinger is a sociable animal and enjoys the company of people. It is intelligent, trustworthy and docile, making it an excellent work pony and safe with children. Haflingers are hardy and require only moderate feeding; however, they do require shelter from cold winds and wet weather. Their most striking feature is their flaxen mane and tail that are usually left long.

Various shades of chestnut, liver or red are permitted, sometimes with a little dappling over paler areas. White patches are undesirable. Height is around 14hh.

The attractive, versatile Haflinger is fast becoming popular in North America. The primary objective of the American Haflinger Registry is to keep the breed pure.

HANOVERIAN

The German Hanoverian horse has a long history. The earliest reference to it as a warhorse was in the 8th century, when Charles Martel frustrated the advances of the Saracens at the Battle of Poitiers. These heavy warhorses were probably a mixture of native, Spanish and Oriental influences.

Hanoverians owe their evolution to warfare, and by the Middle Ages had developed into large, cobby horses, capable of carrying a knight clad in full armor. The type was favored for many centuries, until changes in warfare techniques meant that a lighter horse was eventually required. At this time, the Hanoverian was still a heavy breed, even though it was somewhat taller and more agile than a cob; by the 17th century, three distinctive types were being bred for military purposes: Hanoverian, Mecklenburg and Danish horses.

But it was in the 18th century that the Hanoverian truly came into its own, when a member of the House of Hanover, in the person of George I, ascended the British throne in 1714. He spent much of his reign in Hanover, however, and for the next 100 years or so the Hanoverian was nurtured and improved. English Thoroughbred stallions were bred with Hanoverian mares, and Cleveland Bay bloodlines were also added to produce a horse that was still relatively heavy, but also suitable for farm and coachwork.

There are few breeds whose ancestry has been so well-recorded. This has allowed breeders to trace bloodlines over many generations, improving chances of finding the most promising breeding pairs.

It was George II who established the state stud at Celle in 1735, where horses for agriculture, riding and driving were bred. Here the Hanoverian breed was improved still further, with additions of Trakehner and Thoroughbred blood; the Hanoverian breed registry was founded in 1888.

This horse was very similar to today's famous competition horse. Probably the best known of all the warmbloods, the modern Hanoverian excels in top dressage and showjumping the world over. Nowadays, the Society of Breeders of the Hanoverian Warmblood Horse is responsible for the purity of the breed. Approximately 160 Hanoverians, mostly stallions, are kept by the state and based at Celle, where they are subjected to tests that assess soundness, conformation and character for several months before they are allowed to mate.

The American Hanoverian Society was founded in 1978 to protect the Hanoverian's future role in North American equitation.

The Hanoverian has played a large part in the improvement and formation of other warmblood breeds, such as Westphalian, Mecklenburg and Brandenburg horses. Hanoverians now come in two types: the heavier horses are

used for showjumping, while the lighter ones, which have more of the Thoroughbred in their make-up, are used for dressage.

The Hanoverian is near-perfect in conformation and its Thoroughbred characteristics are immediately discernible. The head is of medium size, with a straight nose and keen, alert eyes and pricked ears. The neck has a graceful arch and is long and muscular, while the chest is well-developed with a deep girth and sloping shoulder. The back is of medium length, with muscular loins and powerful quarters. The legs are strong with large joints, ending in well-shaped hooves.

The most important feature of the Hanoverian, and one of the crucial tests that stallions have to undergo at Celle, is one of character: only horses with an even temperament and a willing disposition are allowed to breed. Hanoverians are noble and proud, with an excellent free-flowing action which allows them to excel at advanced dressage. They come in all solid colors, often with white on the face and legs. They range in height from 15.2–17hh.

HIGHLAND

Like all Scottish native breeds, the Highland has a very ancient history, as indicated by its distinctive dorsal stripe. The foundation breed is Celtic Pony, mixed over the centuries with Galloway – now sadly extinct – plus various European breeds, such as Percheron, Spanish, Barb and Clydesdale. In the 19th century Arab was also added to bring the pony up to today's exacting standards.

The pony is not only native to the Highlands, there is also a smaller variety which inhabits most of the Western Isles. It has always lived and worked with the Scottish crofters and was used in farming, forestry, haulage and general riding, where its equable temperament and sure-footedness were valuable assets. It was also taken to war, used in both the Boer Wars and the First World War.

Even though there has been a stud book for the Highland Pony since the 1880s, no set breed standard exists; consequently, there is a diversity of types and bloodlines. Nevertheless, white marks are frowned upon and stallions with anything other than small stars on their foreheads cannot be registered. The

The Highland Pony has inhabited the north of Scotland for centuries, where it was used in agriculture. More recently. it has also been used for hunting and driving. Scotland's Highland Pony Society dates from 1923.

Highland has proved equally popular in other countries, and there are studs in Europe, Australia, the United States and Canada.

The advent of pony-trekking in the 1950s made the Highland even more popular; this was not only because of its temperament, sturdiness and agility, but also because it could carry up to 210lb with

ease, making it suitable for both adults and children. Today the Highland is used in a number of children's riding events, including jumping, cross-country and pony club games, as well as in long-distance endurance events, showing and driving.

The Highland is a stocky, well-built pony. It has a small, pretty head, with a straight nose, small, often pricked ears, and large kind eyes. It has a strong body with a fairly long, well-developed neck, a neat shoulder, deep girth, and a well-muscled back. The legs are well-boned and sturdy, with hard, shapely hooves and feathering around the fetlocks. The mane and tail are thick and silky and are left long.

Highlands are friendly, with an even temperament and a willingness to work. They are hardy creatures, and although they require a little extra feeding, they are capable of living out in all weathers.

They come in all solid colors, including gray and a variety of shades of fox, cream, gold, yellow and mouse. They can attain a height of up to 14.2hh.

HOLSTEIN

The German Holstein, or Holsteiner, is probably descended from a native breed known as the Marsh Horse, which once roamed the wetlands of the Elbe estuary in what is now Schleswig-Holstein. The Holstein breed dates to the 13th century, when Gerhard I, Count of Holstein and Storman, permitted the monks of the Uetersen monastery to graze their quality horses, which they bred themselves, on private land. These were native stock, that had been mixed with Andalusian, Neapolitan and Oriental blood to produce a heavy, useful horse. This was valued by farmers for its strength and reliability, and as

The horse is God's gift to mankind.

Arabian proverb

a military horse for its courage, stamina, and ability. It was also favored as a coaching horse. After the Reformation, the monastery land was returned to the landowners, who continued the horse-breeding tradition.

By 1686 the Holstein had become so respected that strict guidelines were introduced to protect and improve the breed, which was by now popular throughout Europe. By the 18th century the Holstein's reputation had become so great that vast numbers of horses were exported. Unfortunately, not all of them had been bred to the exacting standards that had once prevailed and general deterioration set in.

By the 19th century, fortunately, the decline had been halted, and measures were now being taken to save and improve the breed. As the demand for warhorses grew less, the Holstein came to be needed as a quality carriage horse, and to this end, Yorkshire Coach Horses and Cleveland Bay stallions were mated with Holstein mares. This was a great success, and the breed was given a new lease of life.

Thoroughbred was also added to refine the breed after the Second World War, which also improved the Holstein's jumping ability and general character. Today, it is a supreme sporthorse, excelling at dressage, showjumping and eventing. It has also been bred to good effect with other warmblood breeds, most effectively with the Hanoverian.

The Holstein is quite different from other warmbloods in that it has a large, rangy build resulting in a huge stride. The head is long and straight with large, flaring nostrils. The ears are expressive and the eyes are large and gentle. The long neck is elegant and well-developed, with high withers; the back is long and straight. The shoulders are shapely and sloping, which also contributes to its long stride. The chest is broad, the girth is deep, and the quarters are slightly sloping, muscular and powerful. The legs are long and muscular.

The Holstein is a fine, well-balanced horse, with an amazing ground-covering, elastic stride. The overall effect is of an elegant horse that carries itself lightly. It is good-natured, obedient and eager to work. Its large size and scope means that it is much in demand as a top-flight competition horse.

They are most commonly bay, though all solid colors, together with gray, are permitted, They stand around 16–17hh.

The quality of Holstein breeding stock is ensured through annual inspections, when horses are evaluated and graded according to quality and to their potential for adding to the breeding pool.

ICELANDIC

Iceland does not have its own indigenous breed of horse. The Icelandic is derived from the Fjord and Døle horses of Norway, and the Celtics, Shetlands, Highlands and Connemaras of the British Isles, which were brought to Iceland by Celts and Vikings in the 9th century. Because of the limited space on board their ships, the invaders would have brought only the best specimens, and once settled, would have allowed their horses to mate freely, producing the Icelandic breed as we know it today. This resulted in a hardy animal, able to tolerate semi-wild conditions and to survive harsh Arctic winters. It was used mainly for farming and for riding over icy terrain.

The Icelandic horse has been bred in closed pedigrees since the Middle Ages, because it must be traceable back to its Icelandic ancestors. Even though it is a pony in stature, it is always referred to as a

horse; this is because there is no word for pony in the Icelandic language. It is often mentioned in the Icelandic Sagas, where to a warrior, a good horse was worth more than gold. Great horses were treated with respect and slain warriors would often have been buried alongside their mounts.

Icelandics have lately been exported to other countries, however, where cross-breeding has been allowed to take place.

It is a well-constructed animal. The head is of medium length, having a typical pony character with small pricked ears and soft, expressive eyes. The neck is well-set, and the chest is broad with a deep girth. The body and legs are stocky and strong and the feet are extremely hard.

The Icelandic is ideal for children, being tough, hardy and happy to live out all-year-round. It has two extra gaits: the *tølt*, which is a running walk with four beats, and is as fast as a canter and very comfortable; and the flying pace, which has two beats and is used for racing, but which makes great demands on horse and rider.

Speeds of up to 30mph can be reached using the flying pace, and to witness this occurring is impressive indeed. The Icelandic is late to mature, however, and should not be backed until it is four years old. It can live to a ripe old age, often working up until 30; in fact, an Icelandic in Britain is known to have died aged 42.

Icelandics come in all solid colors, as well as skewbald, palomino, dun and gray. A silver dapple coat is much prized; this is where the body is a rich brown and the mane and tail appear almost silver by contrast. In winter the coat is very thick, with three distinct layers. Icelandics stand between 12 and 13.2hh, and have been known to reach 14.2hh.

Icelandic horses are usually given names that reflect their color, temperament or other personal traits, often taken from Norse mythology. An example of this would be Grána, meaning 'gray mare', and other Icelandic names might mean 'happy one' or 'the one with frost in his mane'.

IRISH DRAFT

The history of the Irish Draft can be traced back to the Celts, who invaded Ireland, bringing many horses with them, notably Oriental and Spanish breeds, which they mated with their Celtic Ponies. Later, during the Middle Ages, Ireland was settled by the Anglo-Normans, whose much larger, heavier horses would have originated in Europe. These were bred with what was now the Irish Draft to produce a more substantial animal of use to farmers, being capable of plowing, hauling and general riding. It was also used for hunting over Ireland's often difficult terrain.

By the 18th century, improvements had been made to the Irish Draft with additions of Thoroughbred and Arab blood, and Barb and Turkmene bloodlines were also possibly introduced. The end result was a horse with excellent conformation, still capable of heavy work, but an excellent riding horse. It had all the docility and common sense of a heavier, coldblooded breed, but with the sparkle and verve of a hotblooded Arab or Thoroughbred.

During the Potato Famine of 1845–46, Irish Drafts began to diminish in number: Ireland's economy was in a state of turmoil and horse-breeding had almost come to an end. But by the end of the century the

situation had changed for the better, and it was decided that heavier stock, such as Clydesdale and Shire, should be introduced to create a bigger horse. In 1917 a stud book was opened, but by the end of the First World War the breed was once again in jeopardy, as mechanized transport began to be used in farming and haulage. By now, the Irish Draft was predominantly a riding horse, and a hunter in particular.

By the early 20th century, however, more Thoroughbred blood had been added, producing the horse we know today. The breed is still predominantly a hunter, but because it has been mixed with other breeds, particularly the Thoroughbred, it is

now a superb competition horse; it has inherited the Irish Draft's love of jumping, and excels at both cross-country and eventing. A little of the Irish Draft is also present in some steeplechasers.

The head is neat, and its straight nose and medium-length ears gives it a noble mien. The neck is shortish and very strong, the withers are slightly pronounced, and the shoulder is long and sloping. The chest is broad and the girth is deep. The back is

The splendid Irish Draft is predominantly a hunter, but infusions of Arab and Thoroughbred bloodlines have also made it an excellent sporthorse.

medium-length and well-muscled, with strong loins and sloping, powerful quarters. The sturdy, muscular legs have plenty of bone, and the hooves are large and round.

The Irish Draft has all the substance of a medium-weight draft horse, but its hotblood ancestry has produced a refined appearance, with no excess hair on the legs, as in most of the heavier breeds. It has great stamina, agility and courage, and is generally good-natured and willing. It will jump almost anything in sight, but at the same time uses intelligence and common sense.

Most commonly bay, brown, chestnut and gray, Irish Drafts stand somewhere between 15 and 17hh.

JUTLAND HEAVY DRAFT

The Jutland has an ancient and colorful history. It is descended from the coldblooded prehistoric Forest Horse, which much later mated with other indigenous stock to produce a heavy horse. This was the favored mount of knights in armor of the Middle Ages. The breed was further defined when Cleveland Bay and Yorkshire Coach Horse were added to give the horse more substance.

But it was the Suffolk Punch that really made the Jutland Heavy Draft the horse it is today. Steps were taken to improve the breed in around 1850, with the aim of producing a strong horse suitable for the heavy draftwork involved in farming. The breed was developed further in 1862 with the importation of a Suffolk Punch-Shire stallion cross called Oppenheim, which was the ancestor of the greatest Jutland stallion lines, in particular of Aldrup Menkedal, which is now considered the foundation stallion of the breed.

The Jutland has also been influential in the formation of other breeds, such as the Schleswig Heavy Draft and the Danish Warmblood. The stud book of the breed was established in 1881.

The Jutland's head is a little heavy and plain, with a slightly Roman nose. The ears are medium-length and the eyes have a soft, kindly expression. The neck is set high, and is thick, arched and muscular. The withers are rather flat, merging into the broad back. The chest is broad, the girth deep, and the shoulders straight and muscular. The back is short, with rounded loins and hindquarters. The legs are short, stocky and well-boned with plenty of feathering.

Jutlands have plenty of energy and a keen attitude to work, coupled with a kind and calm temperament. They often inherit the trademark chestnut color of the Suffolk Punch, usually with a paler mane and tail. They also come in other solid colors as well as grey and roan. They range in height from 15–16hh.

The Jutland is Denmark's own breed of heavy horse. Its ancestors have been bred on the Jutland Peninsula for as long as anyone can remember.

KABARDIN

The Kabardin is descended from the Tarpan – the wild horse of Eastern Europe and Asia, which sadly became extinct in captivity in 1887. The Kabardin remained unchanged in type until the Russian Revolution when, like many other Russian horses, steps were taken to improve the breed. The original Kabardin was bred with Karabakh, Turkmene, Persian, and Arab to create a much bigger, stronger horse, suitable for riding and general farm work, also for use as a packhorse. The Kabardin is also an excellent mountain horse – possibly the best there is – being sure-footed, agile and intelligent, with the innate ability to search out the safest routes. Its great stamina enables it to work all day without becoming stressed.

The breed remains popular in its place of origin to this day. This is now the Republic of Kabardino-Balkaria, where it is still used for light draft work and for riding. Elsewhere, it is used in competition and to improve other breeds.

The Kabardin is the principal breed of the Northern Caucasus, and is used to improve native stock in Armenia, Azerbaijan, and Georgia. The best Kabardins are raised at the Karachai and Malka studs, and crossings with Thoroughbreds are becoming popular.

The Karbardin has a longish head, often with a slightly Roman nose. The longish ears point inwards and are set close together. The eyes are wise and intelligent and the nostrils flared. The neck is long and well-developed, and the back is straight

and strong; the legs are long and fine, but at the same time also very strong. The overall impression is of a horse with strong Oriental influences.

Kabardins are kind, obedient, intelligent and trustworthy. They are a

God forbid that I should go to any Heaven in which there are no horses.

R.B. Cunninghame Graham, in a letter to Theodore Roosevelt, 1917

hardy breed, and with extra feeding can live out all year. They have strong constitutions and mostly live to a ripe old age.

Colors may be bay, black, brown and very occasionally gray. Height is somewhere between 14.2 and 15.1hh.

KARACABEY

Turkey's native horse population is very large and still plays an integral part in the day-to-day lives of the Turkish people, used for general riding, farm work and for general haulage. Turkey has various types of horses, but the Karacabey is the only one to throw offspring that run consistently true to type.

It is known that the Karacabey is descended from native Turkish stock and it is therefore considered to be the original Turkish horse. The breed itself is a relatively new one, beginning in the 1900s, when native mares were bred with Nonius stallions which the Turks imported from Hungary; Arab was also added in large quantities to refine the breed and to add stamina, agility and speed. Today the Karacabey is still used for light draft work, riding, as a packhorse, and as mounts for the Turkish cavalry.

The head is proud, with a straight nose. The ears are alert and of medium length, and the eyes are kind and intelligent. The neck is quite long and arched, the shoulders sloping, and the girth deep, with a medium-length body, good hindquarters and fine, strong legs.

The Karacabey is a sturdy horse with good stamina and endurance. It is good-natured and is a willing and obedient worker.

It comes in all solid colors, also gray and occasionally roan, and stands somewhere between 15.1 and 16.1hh.

The Karacabey is regarded as the original Turkish horse, in that it is descended from native stock.

KNABSTRUP

The Knabstrup's origins go back 200 years or so, but its ancestry can be traced back even further, possibly to prehistoric Iberian horses. The Knabstrup is unusual for a European horse in that it has a distinctive spotted coat. This is thought to have been inherited from its prehistoric forebears, many of which can be seen depicted in ancient cave paintings.

Spotted horses were very popular at the courts of European royalty in the 16th and 17th centuries; but the Knabstrup was founded much later, in the early 1800s, when an Iberian mare of the Knabstrup Estate in Denmark was mated with a palomino Frederiksborg stallion. The foal was born

Far back, far back in our dark soul the horse prances . . . The horse, the horse! The symbol of surging potency and power of movement, of action . . .

D.H. Lawrence

with a spotted coat of many colors, which also had an attractive sheen. This horse became the foundation stallion of the Knabstrup breed.

Unfortunately, because subsequent horses were bred primarily for their unusual coats, insufficient care and attention was given to their conformation, leading to gradual deterioration, when the breed subsequently lost its popularity and almost disappeared. However, the horse has been improved in recent years, and the addition of Thoroughbred bloodlines has made it popular once more. Today it is used as a general riding horse and also features in showing classes and even circuses, due to its spotted coat.

The head is large, with a straight or Roman nose. The ears are small and well-pricked and the eyes have a kind, gentle expression. The muzzle is square, with large, open nostrils. The neck is high-set, the shoulders are well-developed, and the chest is broad. The back is rather long, with slightly sloping quarters, and the legs are strong with plenty of good bone. The mane and tail are rather sparse.

With its excellent natural paces, the Knabstrup is a good-quality riding horse. It is complaisant and intelligent, easy to train, and is an obedient and willing worker.

Colors and patterns are various, with permutations similar to those present in the Appaloosa. Full leopard spotting is the most highly prized, though one overall color or roan is also possible. Height is 15.2hh.

In 1971, the Knabstrup received an influx of Appaloosa blood. This was a logical step, in that the Appaloosa derived directly from the spotted horses brought to the New World by the conquistadors from Spain.

LIPIZZANER

The Lipizzaner is probably one of the world's most recognizable breeds due to its association with the Spanish Riding School of Vienna. Despite its origins in what is now Slovenia, the Lipizzaner has a far more ancient history, dating back to the 8th century and the Moorish occupation of Spain. The Moors brought horses of Oriental origin to Spain, such as Arabs and Barbs. These were bred with the heavier Iberian horses, which in turn produced the Andalusian – the most important element in the Lipizzaner's line of heredity.

In 1580 Archduke Charles, son of the Holy Roman Emperor Ferdinand I, who had inherited Austria-Hungary, sought to improve his horses, and decided on the system of *haute école*, or the practice of

The wind of heaven is that which blows between a horse's ears.

Arabian Proverb

advanced classical dressage. He founded a stud at Lipizza for the purpose, which also specialized in breeding carriage horses, and filled it with quality Spanish (Iberian) horses, known to be capable of the discipline. He used these horses as the foundation stock of the Lipizzaner, crossing them with heavier native breeds, together with Barb, Arab, Andalusian, Neapolitan and Kladruber. Thus, over a period of several hundred years, the classic riding horse was born.

The illustrious Spanish Riding School had been founded in Vienna in 1572. It got

RIGHT: A celebrated dancing Lipizzaner at the Spanish Riding School in Vienna.

OPPOSITE: A Lipizzaner stallion at stud.

its name, not because of its Spanish riding traditions but because of the Spanish origins of its horses. The aim of the school was to teach the art of classical equestrianism to men of noble breeding. The original venue had been a crude wooden structure, which was eventually replaced by the splendid building that was comissioned by Charles VI in 1735 and which is still in use today. The Spanish Riding School is now stocked exclusively with Lipizzaner stallions.

When the Austro-Hungarian Empire collapsed, the stud was moved to Piber in Austria, and during the Second World War was evacuated to Germany for its own protection. Today, Lipizzaners are bred mainly at Piber (which supplies all the stallions for the Spanish Riding School), though some also come from Lipizza and Babolna in Hungary, and from the Czech Republic, Slovenia and Romania. Nowadays, as well as performing in the Spanish Riding School, Lipizzaners are also used as draft horses, for carriage driving, and are becoming popular as general riding horses.

The Lipizzaner breed was based on six foundation stallions, and their different characteristics can be seen in their descendants to this day. Lipizzaners can therefore vary according to which of the six bloodlines were used, but generally speaking they are of an Iberian type, similar to the Lusitano and Andalusian.

The head is large with either a straight or Roman nose. The ears are finely pointed and alert and the eyes kind and intelligent. The neck is well-set, powerful and well-muscled with a good crest. The chest is wide with a deep girth. The shoulders can be slightly straight and short. The back is long but strong and muscular, with powerful quarters and a slightly low-set tail. The legs

Lipizzaner foals are born with dark coats, which turn to a sparkling white as they reach maturity.

are shortish but powerful, with small, well-shaped, tough hooves.

The noble Lipizzaner possesses all the admirable qualities of its breeding: the agility and balance of its Iberian forebears, as well as the stamina and refinement of the Orientals. It combines stamina with natural balance and agility, is kind, intelligent, willing and obedient, but with plenty of sparkle. Lipizzaners are late to mature, usually around the age of 7, and should not be worked too young. However, they remain sound for a relatively long time and usually live to a good age.

Lipizzaners are famous for their gray (white) coats. Foals are born dark, but most lighten to become pure white on reaching maturity. Very few remain brown or black. They stand between 15 and 15.3hh.

Some non-white Lipizzaners have traditionally been kept at the Spanish Riding School as reminders of the white Lipizzaners' bay, black, brown or roan Spanish forebears.

LUSITANO

The Lusitano shares its heritage with the Andalusian, both having been descended from the Iberian riding horse. The Lusitano gets its name (adopted only in the early 20th century) from Lusitania, which was the Roman name for Portugal. The origins of the breed date to around 25,000 BC and to the ancient ancestors of the Sorraia pony, which can be seen in cave paintings throughout the Iberian Peninsula.

Unlike the Andalusian, the Lusitano's breeding has remained truer to its Sorraia ancestry, in that it has only received infusions of Oriental, Garrano and Spanish blood. To keep the breed true to type, this mix hasn't been changed for centuries and care is taken to use only horses with obvious Iberian characteristics.

The Lusitano was bred mainly for agricultural use around the fertile River Tagus, where it is still used for the purpose. It is also used in bullfighting, as well as in *haute école*. Thankfully, in Portugal, the bull is not killed, and the entire business takes place with the rider on the horse's back. However, the Lusitano has to be incredibly agile and fast to avoid injury.

These horses are highly prized and receive *haute école* training to enhance their precision so that they can survive the demanding and dangerous spectacle. The Lusitano stallions are trained to these high standards before they are sent to stud, and all fighting horses are left entire; it is believed that geldings lack the courage and intelligence to work in the bullring.

Today, the horse is also used in lower levels of dressage. Infusions of Lusitano are also used to improve other breeds.

The Portuguese Lusitano shares much of its ancestry with the Spanish Andalusian.

166

The Lusitano has a fine, noble countenance. The head is quite long, with a straight or slightly Roman nose and flared nostrils. The ears are of medium length, well-shaped and alert. The eyes are keen and intelligent, the neck is set high, with a well-developed muscular crest and well-defined withers. The sloping shoulders are powerful and the chest is broad with a deep girth. The back is short and strong and the loins broad, with quarters that are not too large. The Lusitano's high-stepping action is attributed to its strong, long hocks, which are capable of great impulsion, and the deep flexion is achieved by a well-developed second thigh (stifle).

This noble and courageous horse is kind, good-natured and obedient. It is level-headed and not given to sudden panic, which are important attributes in a fighting horse.

They may be any solid color as well as gray, and they stand between 15 and 16hh.

The Lusitano is a talented dressage horse, having a natural high-stepping action that is most attractive.

171

MAREMMANA

The foundation of the Maremmana horse, from the Tuscan region of Maremma, originally rested on the now-extinct Neapolitan horse, with later infusions of Andalusian and other European stock. Over the centuries, however, the breed was weakened by matings with local semi-wild horses and other horses or ponies that appeared in the vicinity. Thoroughbred has more recently been added; this has greatly improved quality, though the Maremmana's hardiness has suffered as a result.

Today the Maremmana is still used on farms and as a general riding horse; it is also used by the Italian mounted police.

The Maremmana's head is rather plain and workmanlike, with a straight or slightly Roman nose. The neck is short, with a straight shoulder, flat withers and a low-set tail. The legs, however, are strong and sturdy, with good tough hooves.

The Maremmana is a resilient animal with a calm temperament. It is reliable, obedient and willing to work. Coats may be any color, including gray and roan. Height is usually between 15 and 15.3hh.

Maremmanas, though not known for their turn of speed, were the traditional mounts of Tuscan cattlemen.

MÉRENS

Horses that were remarkably similar to the Mérens pony have roamed the Andorran Pyrenees since prehistoric times, and can be found depicted in the ancient cave paintings at Niaux. The native breed has changed slightly over the years, having been interbred with heavy horses brought by the Romans to the region, and with Oriental bloodlines later on.

The Mérens's stamina and sure-footedness has made it eminently suitable for the inhospitable terrain, and mountain farmers have been using it for plowing and hauling for hundreds of years. The Mérens was also used for transporting lumber – also by the military in the Middle Ages and by Napoleon during his campaigns.

The Mérens, or Ariègeois, is similar to the British Dales and Fell ponies and the Friesian horse. Breeders still raise their stock the traditional way: the ponies live out all-year-round and the foals are born during the early spring snows. In summer, transhumance occurs, when the ponies are herded up high into the mountains. They are allowed their freedom for several months, before individuals are selected for breaking, breeding or selling on. Today they are still used for farming, forestry, driving, and also as children's ponies.

The Mérens is a most attractive pony, with a small, neat head, a slightly dished or straight nose, small pricked ears, and kind, soft eyes. The neck is short and well-developed, and the body strong and stocky, with well-developed hindquarters. The legs are shortish, with plenty of bone, and there is a little feathering around the fetlocks.

Well-balanced, level-headed and compliant, the Mérens is highly energetic, and being tough, it can withstand the harshest conditions. Usually black, it stands somewhere between 13 and 14.2hh.

The Mérens pony has been used by Pyrenean farmers for hundreds of years.

NEW FOREST

The New Forest Pony is probably a descendant of the Celtic Pony, as are all the British native breeds, though the earliest mention of it was in the time of King Canute (c.995–1035), famous for ordering back the sea's incoming tide.

The New Forest is in the county of Hampshire in southern England and consists mainly of scrubland, bog and moorland, which has led to the development of a hardy animal, designed to survive harsh conditions. Over the years, Thoroughbred and Arab blood were introduced, mainly to increase size and performance and to improve the pony's appearance, but is was not until the end of the 19th century, during the reign of Queen Victoria, that a structured breeding program was initiated. At the same time, other British breeds were also introduced, such as Dartmoor, Exmoor, Welsh, Fell, Dales and Highland ponies.

In 1891, the Society for the Improvement of New Forest Ponies was founded to ensure that there was an ample supply of quality stallions living in the New Forest and this in turn led to the official publication of the first stud book in 1910. Nowadays, although still living and

The substitution of the internal combustion engine for the horse marked a very gloomy milestone in the progress of mankind.

Sir Winston Churchill

breeding in their home environment, many quality ponies are also bred in private studs all over the world.

The New Forest Pony is one of the larger breeds native to Britain. It is an ideal child's or teenager's pony and excellent for driving. It has a well-proportioned body that is more slender than other British breeds, and well-formed feet.

The ponies are calm, good-natured and a pleasure to own – substantial enough for dressage, showjumping and cross-country; in fact, it is often said that a good New Forest Pony can rise to any occasion.

Coats can be any color, with touches of white, while height is in the range of 12–14.2hh.

Ponies such as these have grazed the common land of the New Forest for many hundreds of years.

NORIKER

The Noriker is also known as the South German Coldblood, the Pinzgauer, and the Oberlander. The breed is an ancient one, dating to the days of the Roman Empire, when several heavy breeds, possibly with Andalusian and Neapolitan blood flowing in their veins, were introduced to the province; this now equates with modern Austria, but was then known to the Romans as Noricum.

The breed which developed from these heavy horses was strong and sure-footed, making it ideal for draft work in difficult mountain conditions, where it was used for farming and forestry. By the 16th century,

an infusion of Andalusian and Neapolitan bloodlines had been introduced, which brought a degree of finesse and agility to the breed. A South German strain had developed by the 19th century, and this was improved by the addition of Norman, Cleveland Bay, Holstein, Hungarian, Clydesdale and Oldenburg, which made the breed much lighter and more elegant.

Today there are five different types of Noriker, all of which are lightish draft horses, still used for farming in Austria and Germany.

The Noriker's head is medium-sized and rather plain, with a straight or slightly Roman nose. The neck is short, well-developed and strong, and the shoulder is

straight. The body is sturdy with sloping quarters and a low-set tail. The legs are short and sturdy, with hard hooves and a little feathering.

The Noriker's breeding has made it active and agile. It is strong and its sure-footedness makes it suitable for difficult terrain. It is amenable and obedient and copes well with harsh conditions.

Most commonly chestnut, Norikers often have a flaxen mane and tail. They can also be bay, brown, black, roan and spotted, and stand somewhere between 15.1 and 16.2hh.

The Noriker is still used for farming in Austria and Germany.

NORTH SWEDISH

Another breed linked to the prehistoric Celtic Pony, the North Swedish also shares its ancestry with the Norwegian Døle, and has Friesian, Norfolk Trotter, Heavy Draft and Thoroughbred in its make-up. The breed subsequently split into two distinctive types: the lighter version, known as the North Swedish Trotter, is capable of covering 0.62 mile (1km) in 1 minute 30 seconds, which is faster than many other breeds, recognized for their speed, can accomplish.

The heavier draft type is of greater stature and is used for general farm and haulage work.

Like the Døle, the breed resembles a large pony. The head is small and neat, with a broad forehead, a straight or slightly Roman nose, and a squarish muzzle. The ears are small and alert and the eyes kind but inquisitive. The neck is short and well-developed with a slight crest. The chest and shoulders are powerful, the girth is deep, and the back is long, with well-muscled hindquarters. The legs are short but sturdy, with good bone, hard hooves, and

feathering around the heels. The heavier type has rather more bone and substance.

The North Swedish is tough, hardy and can expect a long life. It requires little care and feeding and has great stamina and endurance. It has a well-balanced, springy action, and the trotting type has a particularly good turn of speed.

Any color is permitted and height is around 15.1hh.

Like the Døle-Gudbrandsdal of Norway, the North Swedish has the appearance of a pony but is in fact classified as a horse.

NORTHLANDS

The Northlands is uncommon outside its home territory of Norway. Like most of the native breeds of Northern Europe, it can trace its ancestry back to the prehistoric Celtic Pony, although Tarpan blood is somewhere in its make-up.

It resembles the Shetland Pony of Scotland, and although it was bred by farmers, with no particular thought of keeping the breed pure, it has remained remarkably true to type for hundreds of years. The Northland was under serious threat by the 1940s, when numbers dropped to only 43. But due to the work of breeders, and a well-bred stallion called Rimfaske, the Northlands has been saved from extinction.

Today, with riding fast increasing in popularity and the demand for ponies growing, the breed is on the increase and is out of immediate danger. The Northland makes an excellent children's pony and is still used for light work around local farms.

The Northland's head is usually in proportion to its body, but can occasionally be a little on the large side. The ears are small and neat, and the eyes large and kind. The neck is strong and of medium length; the body is longish and the legs sturdy, with hard hooves and a little feathering around the fetlocks.

Northlands are tough and hardy and can live out all-year-round in the harshest of conditions, requiring the minimum of extra food and care. It is an energetic breed, which makes it fun to ride.

Colors are bay, brown, chestnut and gray, and height is somewhere between 13.2 and 14.2hh.

The Northlands pony is largely confined to its native Norway, and like other such Northern European breeds, is descended from the Celtic Pony.

OLDENBURG

Bred originally as coach horses, Oldenburgs are the heaviest of the modern German warmbloods. It dates from the early part of the 17th century, when Count Anton Guenther initiated a program for the breed.

The Oldenburg's earliest ancestors were heavy Friesian horses that were infused with Spanish and Arabian bloodlines. The breed was stabilized in the 19th century by introduction of Thoroughbred, Cleveland Bay, Yorkshire Coach Horse, Anglo-Norman and Hanoverian bloodlines.

The Oldenburg was also used by the military as a strong artillery horse. As the

What do we, as a nation, care about books? How much do you think we spend altogether on our libraries, public or private, as compared with what we spend on our horses?

John Ruskin

years passed, however, the need for such horses began to diminish. It was replaced by a demand for a lighter riding horse, suitable for pleasure and competition.

In the second half of the 20th century, bloodlines of lighter horses were again introduced, such as Thoroughbred, Trakehner, Hanoverian and Westphalian. Nowadays, the Oldenburg excels at dressage and showjumping; it retains its ability as a coach or carriage horse, however, and is used for the purpose to this day.

The Oldenburg is distinguished by its noble head and proud, workmanlike air. It

has a high-set neck, long shoulder, strong back, and a well-muscled croup with strong joints. It can be used not only as an elegant dressage horse, but also as a powerful showjumper, having a large frame and a long, active stride.

The Oldenburg resembles a hunter type. Its character is equable, making it pleasant to handle and ride. It is usually black, bay or brown, and stands between 16.2 and 17.2hh.

From humble beginnings as a coach horse, the Oldenburg has evolved into a very capable modern sporthorse.

ORLOV TROTTER

The Orlov, or Orloff, Trotter is one of the foremost breeds of its type in the world. It was founded in the 18th century by Count Alexey Orlov, whose ambition was to produce a superb trotting horse. He founded a stud at Ostrov, near Moscow, for the purpose, bringing in a large number of Arab horses. One of these was the stallion Smetanka, a silver-gray horse, large and rather long-backed for the breed, with an extravagant trot. After a season, Orlov was left with a few progeny, bred from Dutch Harddraver, Mecklenburg, Danish, Thoroughbred and Arabian mares.

Orlov decided to look for a better stud farm, with more grazing, which he found in Khrenovoye in the Voronezh region to the

The winged coursers harness'd to the car;
Xanthos and Balios of immortal breed,
Sprung from the wind, and like the
wind in speed.
Whom the wing'd harpy, swift
Podarge, bore,
By Zephyr pregnant on the breezy shore.

From the Iliad of Homer
(Xanthos and Balios were Achilles's horses)

south of Moscow. He considered it perfect for his purpose, having vast areas of grassland, clear springs, and a dry climate.

The Khrenovoye Stud was thus founded in 1778, and the following year produced a colt called Polkan I, which in turn was mated with a Danish mare carrying Spanish blood. The result was a foal called Bars I, which eventually showed exceptional stamina and trotting abilities and became the foundation stallion of the Orlov breed.

The Orlov is a muscular horse, famous for its exceptional and impressive action. Its stamina and quality ensured that it reigned supreme on the race track until the end of the 19th century, when Standardbreds and later French Trotters were introduced to the scene. Unfortunately, the Orlov is now in crisis, which is largely due to the introduction of these faster breeds.

The Orlov has a small, elegant head, with a noble profile and ears highly reminiscent of the Arab horse. The hindquarters are powerful, and like many trotters, the shoulders are straight. It is energetic, sure-footed and bold. Owing to its swift, balanced trot, it is suitable for riding and driving as well as trotting.

Orlovs are usually gray, black or bay and range from 15.2–17hh in height.

Leo Tolstoy, the author of War and Peace, *immortalized one such exceptional trotter in his novella,* Kholstomer *(Strider):* The Story of a Horse,

PERCHERON

The Percheron comes from La Perche in Normandy in Northern France. The breed is an ancient one, dating back to 732, when Arab horses, abandoned by the Saracens after their defeat at the Battle of Poitiers, were allowed to breed with the local heavy mares of the region. The Percheron type was the result.

At this time, the horse was much lighter than its modern counterpart and was used for riding as well as for light draft work. The type remained popular until the Middle Ages and the Crusades, when Arab and Barb horses from the Holy Land were mated with Percherons. It was also around this time that the Comte de Perche brought back Spanish horses from his forays in Spain; these were also mated with the Percheron, with further infusions of Andalusian added later on.

By the 18th century, the original breed had become almost completely eradicated by additions of Thoroughbred and more Arab; in 1820 two gray Arab stallions were mated with Percheron mares, thus creating the predominantly gray color of the modern-day breed.

By now all the heaviness of the ancient breed had disappeared; consequently, heavy mares from other regions were bred with Percheron stallions to make them more suitable for agriculture and to formulate the breed as it is known today. The lighter Percheron still exists and is used as a heavy

The Percheron has had a large part to play in France's long history.

riding horse, while the heavy version is still used for farm and forestry work and, in some countries, for pulling drays. It is also popular in the show ring.

Over the years the Percheron has been heavily exported to other countries, such as the U.K., Canada, Australia and other parts of Europe, which has helped in its recognition as one of the world's leading heavy breeds.

The Percheron's head is proud and elegant, for a heavy breed, with a straight nose, broad forehead, expressive eyes, and short, shapely ears. The neck is short to medium, well-developed and with great strength. The shoulders are nicely sloping and well-shaped, with a broad chest and a deep girth. The Percheron is fairly short in the back, which adds to its strength, with slightly sloping but broad quarters. The legs are short and sturdy, with well-shaped tough hooves with very little feather.

The Percheron possesses a good deal of elegance due to the large amounts of Arab blood that have been added over the centuries. It has an excellent temperament, is calm, obedient and easy to handle, and has a keen intelligence. It has a smooth but lively action, which makes it comfortable to ride.

Mainly gray, Percherons can be occasionally black or dark chestnut. There are two types: the small Percheron, which stands between 14.1 and 16.1hh and the large, which is somewhere between 16.1 and 17.3hh.

SELLE FRANÇAIS

Many of the best-known breeds are a fusion of several others and the Selle Français is no exception. Breeders of this beautiful warmblood had been working for many years in their quest for the ultimate competition horse, and used a variety of breeds to achieve their goal. Finally, in the 1950s, the breed was given official status and was named the Selle Français or French Saddle Horse.

Its main ancestor is the Norman, dating back to the Middle Ages, which itself was a cross between indigenous mares and imported horses, such as Arabs and other Orientals. The Norman's primary use haad been as a warhorse, but the line had

Stand, Bayard, stand! - the steed obeyed,
With arching neck and bending head,
And glancing eye and quivering ear,
As if he loved his lord to hear.

Walter Scott (From the Lady of the Lake)

also been influenced by German and Danish carthorses, along with the Thoroughbred and Norfolk Roadster. Other infusions, such as Limousin, Charentais and Vendéen, have also played their part in the production of the modern Selle Français.

It was mainly the Thoroughbred, however, which was responsible for the athletic horse we know today. It now excels at competition, eventing and hunting, and is a particularly talented showjumper.

The Selle Français is an elegant horse. The standard demands a fine head, sloping shoulders, and well-sprung ribs. The legs should be strong and the hindquarters powerful. There are up to five different weights to suit individual tastes.

Like many of the warmblood breeds, the Selle Français has an even, placid temperament, but is intelligent, willing and energetic enough for top competition.

Its color is mainly chestnut, although others are acceptable. It stands somewhere between 15 and 17hh.

The French have a long and distinguished history of horse-breeding, the Selle Français being only one of their many triumphs. It is one of the finest of today's sporthorses.

SHAGYA ARABIAN

The Shagya Arabian comes from Hungary's second most famous breeding establishment, the Babolna Stud, founded in the late 1700s; the other is the Mezöhegyes Stud.

In 1816 the military stipulated that all brood mares should be bred with Oriental stallions to provide cavalry and harness horses; stallions with mixed Oriental blood as well as Iberian crosses were also used. The results, although fairly lightweight, were horses that were tough and had a good deal of stamina.

Following this success, it was decided that the Bobolna Stud should concentrate on breeding horses with predominantly Arab blood, which was the beginning of the excellent Shagya Arabian.

Today's breed is descended from one Arab stallion, called Shagya, which was brought from Syria in 1836. He was fairly large for an Arab, standing at 15.2¹/2hh, and was from the Siglavi or Seglawy strain. The stallion was typically Arab in conformation, with a fine dished nose, a proud high-crested neck, a short body, and a high-set tail. It was mated with the military-style mares to produce the first Shagya Arabians and subsequent breeding by selection has produced a beautiful, refined riding horse of the highest possible quality. Today Shagya Arabians make excellent riding and competition horses and are also used for driving. They remain popular in their native land, but are relatively rare elsewhere.

The Shagya is very like the Arab in conformation, but a little heavier. The head is wedge-shaped, with a wide forehead and a straight or dished nose. The ears are neatly pointed and alert, and the eyes are kind. The muzzle is small and delicate, with large flaring nostrils. The neck is beautifully arched, well-muscled, and set high. The shoulders are sloping, with a broad chest and deep girth; the body is fairly short, with well-defined quarters and long, elegant legs; well-muscled at the top, the legs have more bone than those of the traditional Arab.

The Shagya has the constitution of the Arab but is bigger and stronger. It is kind, noble and spirited, and has great stamina, speed and agility.

All solid colors are acceptable, though many have inherited the Shagya stallion's gray color. Rarest of all is black. They stand somewhere between 14.2 and 15.2hh.

The action of the Shagya, like that of all Arabians, is unique. It is free and elastic as though it were moving on springs.

SHETLAND

The Shetland, probably related to the Celtic Pony, is possibly the most famous of the small breeds.

The Shetlands are 100 or so offshore islands, lying off the northern coast of Scotland. The islands are remote and have a harsh climate, particularly in winter. There is not much shelter for the ponies that inhabit the islands. Food is scarce, but they have adapted to survive on very little. They live on next to nothing during the winter months, but it is known that they come down from the hills to feed on the seaweed that has been washed up on the beaches.

It is unclear where these Shetlands originated, but there is evidence from Bronze Age remains that they have been present for a very long time, probably descended from the Celtic Pony. Alternatively, they may have crossed the ice from Scandinavia, or may even have come from Europe.

Traditionally, Shetlands were used by islanders as riding, plowing, pack and harness ponies. In 1870, the Londonderry Stud at Bressay, Scotland, fixed the type and character of the breed and today's best stock can still be traced to the famous Londonderry sires, even though the stud no longer exists.

The Shetland Pony Stud Book Society was started in 1890 to maintain purity and encourage high-quality animals.

The Shetland's head is small and neat and can be slightly dished. The ears are small and the eyes open and bold. The neck, shoulders and withers are well-defined; the chest and quarters must be strong and muscular. The mane and tail is profuse, with straight feathering on the legs. The coat is double-layered – a feature unique to the Shetland Pony.

The Shetland has plenty of character and can be willful on occasions. Because it is relatively strong for its size, unless it has been properly trained and has good manners, it may be too much for a small child. However, when kept in a suitable environment, with adult help on hand, Shetlands make superb children's ponies.

Shetlands can be most colors, and black, brown, bay, chestnut, gray, piebald and skewbald are all common.

Standard Shetlands grow to a maximum height of 42 inches (107cm). Since the 1980s, however, a miniature Shetland has been developed; this does not exceed 34 inches.

SHIRE

The English Shire is one of the most famous and distinctive of all the draft horses and one of the largest and most majestic breeds in the world. Descended from medieval warhorses, whose immense strength enabled them to carry knights into battle wearing full armor, it was probably based on the Friesian horse, with later infusions of Brabant. It was brought to England by the Dutch to drain the fens of East Anglia. However, it was not until the late 19th century that the best heavy horses in England were selected to develop the breed as it is known today.

The Shire's strength also made it suitable for agriculture and heavy haulage work, so initially the breed was established in Lincolnshire and Cambridgeshire, where strong horses were required to cope with heavy fenland soil; but the Shire soon became widespread in Staffordshire, Leicestershire and Derbyshire, until it eventually spread over England as a whole.

Up until the 1930s, the Shire was widely seen across the country, but numbers dropped dramatically when mechanization of farming began to appear, putting the breed in danger of disappearing altogether. Fortunately, the problem was detected by a few dedicated breeders, who helped to promote the breed and restore it to its former glory.

The Shire Horse Society has worked tirelessly to raise funds and encourage the spread of the breed to other countries. Today, there are active Shire Horse societies across Europe, the United States, Canada and Australia. Although a few Shires are still used on farms today, they are kept mainly for the sheer pleasure of working

OPPOSITE: Shires are descended from medieval warhorses.

ABOVE: Though rare, Shires are occcasionally used on the farm: this one is turning hay.

RIGHT: A Shire mare and foal.

them in their traditional roles. They are also used in plowing competitions, again, for pleasure, and for the same reason, are used in pairs by breweries to deliver beer locally; the spectacle obviously makes for excellent publicity.

The Shire's most significant feature is its sheer size and massive muscular

197

conformation. It is the largest and strongest horse in the world and weighs a ton or more when mature. Built ultimately for strength, the chest is wide, the back short-coupled, the loins and quarters massive. The legs, joints and feet are sufficiently large to balance and support the Shire's weight; the lower legs are covered with long, straight, silky feathers. In the show ring, white feathers are generally preferred as they help to accentuate the horse's action. Even though the Shire is such a large horse, it is not an ungainly heavyweight; in fact it is very much in proportion and quite awesome to behold. The head is always noble, the nose slightly Roman, and the eyes are large and wise.

The Shire is well-known for its patient, gentle and placid nature; it is a true 'gentle giant'. In fact, it is quite amazing that such a strong animal weighing so much can be so easily handled, and it is not uncommon to see them ridden or handled by children or small women. Its kindness is legendary.

Black, brown and gray are the recognized colors of the breed. White feathers on the legs are preferred for the show ring, and white face markings are common. They stand somewhere between 16.2 and 18hh.

The Shire is believed to be a survivor of an early type described by medieval writers as the 'Great Horse' of England. This may have been a development of the British 'War Horse', whose immense strength and courage was described by chroniclers of the Roman legions, after Julius Caesar, seeking to encompass Britain within the Roman Empire, landed on Britain's shores in 55 BC.

SORRAIA

The Sorraia was discovered in Iberia by a Portuguese zoologist, Ruy d'Andrade, in 1920, when he was fascinated to learn that a subspecies of wild horse was alive and well in Europe. Many disputed that it was a true wild horse, and some thought it impossible that one could have survived in a pure state, having made no contact with horses that man had already had a hand in breeding.

When Andrade researched further into the genetics of the Sorraia, he found that it had a similar skull and teeth to those of the Andalusian and Lusitano. He therefore concluded that the Sorraia was the wild ancestor of both of these breeds.

The Sorraia owes its existence as a possible wild species to the inaccessibility of its habitat in the lowland wilderness bordering the Sorraia river, after which it was named.

The Sorraia is a light-colored pony with a dorsal stripe along the back and zebra stripes on the legs. Due to its rarity, inbreeding has been intense; however, this has not affected its hardiness. At first glance, the Sorraia seems to bear a slight resemblance to the Lusitano.

Like many of the world's wild horses, the Sorraia is independent and hardy. It is able to survive on the most meager pasture and can do without shelter in winter. It is an excellent packhorse. Usually dun or gray, height is between 12.2 and 13.2hh.

SUFFOLK PUNCH

The Suffolk Horse, usually known as the Suffolk Punch, originated in East Anglia in England. It takes its name from the county of Suffolk, while 'punch' is an old word meaning short and thickset. It is thought to date back to 1506 and is the oldest heavy breed in Britain.

The breed was first developed by crossing the native heavy mares of the region with imported French Norman stallions. However, modern-day Suffolks can be traced back on the male side to a single, nameless stallion, foaled in 1768 and belonging to Thomas Crisp of Orford, near Woodbridge, Suffolk. Even though the breed is relatively pure, infusions of Norfolk Trotter, Thoroughbred and cob were added during the centuries that followed.

Immensely strong, it is also quite agile, due to its relatively small size. These qualities, combined with a lack of feather on the legs, like the Percheron, made it ideal for working the heavy clay soils of East Anglia. Moreover, its small food consumption, in proportion to its size, enabled it to work for

long days on the farm without stopping.

As with many of the heavy breeds, numbers fell dangerously low when farm tractors became widespread. Today, Suffolks are rare, even though there has been a concerted effort to increase numbers in recent years. Today, Suffolks are shown, used in plowing competitions, or are kept by breweries for their novelty value.

The Suffolk Punch is always chestnut in color (the traditional spelling in this instance is chesnut, without the 't'). The breed is well-known for its great strength, and its extremely powerful, muscular body, with relatively short legs, provides a low center of gravity; this enables the horse to pull plows or vehicles that much more easily. Suffolks mature early and can do light work when they are 2 years old. They continue working well into their 20s.

The Suffolk is docile and hardworking. It is capable of almost any kind of work and is easy to maintain. Height is between 16.1 and 17.1hh.

While the great warhorses of medieval times were still locked in mortal combat on the battlefield, East Anglian farmers were quietly developing their very own breed of heavy horse – the Suffolk Punch.

SWEDISH WARMBLOOD

Like many European warmbloods, the Swedish Warmblood was developed to produce a supreme cavalry horse, with strength, stamina, intelligence and courage.

In the 17th century, the Royal Stud at Flyinge mated indigenous coldblooded stock with many European breeds, most specifically Iberian, Friesian, Barb and Arab. This produced the breed's foundation stock and a stud book for the Swedish Warmblood was eventually opened in 1874.

It was necessary for horses to undergo stringent tests before they could be registered to ensure that their conformation was up to standard; action, stamina, temperament and performance were also rigorously tested.

Over the next 100 years or so, the breed was refined and improved with infusions of Hanoverian, Trakehner, English Thoroughbred and more Arab. Therefore, it could be almost said that the quality warmblood we know today was especially designed for the purpose, that is, to excel at competition; this includes dressage, eventing, showjumping and carriage-driving.

The head is rather fine and long, with a straight nose and a well-defined muzzle with flared nostrils. The ears are long, giving an impression of alertness, and the eyes are bright and intelligent. The neck is long and elegant with a well-developed crest. The shoulders are muscular and sloping, with a good broad chest and deep girth. The back is medium-length, with strong loins and well-developed quarters. The long legs are muscular with large joints and the hooves are strong and shapely.

These horses are respected for their jumping ability and excellent paces. They are willing, obedient and intelligent and have a lively, spirited demeanor.

They may be any solid color and usually stand between 16.1 and 17hh.

The Swedish Warmblood Association of North America (SWANA) was established in the 1980s.

TERSKY

The Tersky or Tersk is a true performance horse, specializing in endurance, racing, jumping and dressage. Not only has it excellent sporting and athletic capabilities, it is also one of the most beautiful of the Russian breeds.

Originating in the Northern Caucasus, the breed is now concentrated at the Stavropol Stud. Breeding and rearing previously took place on the steppes, with the result that weaker stock succumbed to wolves or died of disease. Learning to survive, therefore, made the breed tough.

The modern breed is a product of the early 20th century; it was based on the Strelets Arab, produced by crossing Anglo-Arabs with Orlovs, and was developed by crossing Arabs with old-type Terskys to which Thoroughbred blood had been also introduced.

There are three variations on the Tersky: the first is lightweight, fine and Arab-like in appearance, and is known as the Eastern type. The second is middleweight, sturdier and longer in the back, with a frame that is thicker-set, while the third is the heavier type that has received infusions of Trakehner.

The Tersky is a horse of medium height and great beauty, reflecting its Arabian heritage. The head is finely formed with a dished profile; the eyes are large and intelligent and the nostrils flared.

The Tersky has an equable temperament. It combines kindness and intelligence with courage and stamina.

They are predominantly gray, usually with a metallic sheen to the coat, while black, chestnut and bay are also possible. They stand between 15 and 16hh.

The Tersky is the ultimate sporthorse, having the stamina, grace and beauty of the Arab.

THOROUGHBRED

The Thoroughbred is probably the most important breed of all and is the best known of all the British breeds. Its history dates to the 17th century, when English farmers and landowners became increasingly interested in racing. Until that time, local horses, not been specifically bred for the purpose, were being raced, and it soon became apparent that a selective breeding program was required to make them more suitable for the task. This became more urgent as gambling became popular with the public at large.

The wealthier landowners realized that while the native horses had stamina, they were lacking in speed, so between 1689 and 1729, in order to improve the stock, they began to import horses from the Middle East. It is generally accepted that the modern Thoroughbred stems from three such stallions: the Byerley Turk, the Darley Arabian and the Godolphin Arabian, all of which had a long experience of working at stud. Between them, they established the three bloodlines of Herod, Eclipse and Matchem, which were pivotal to the British Thoroughbred – a name not applied to the breed until 1821.

Although initially bred with racing in mind, the qualities of the Thoroughbred make it an ideal horse for all other equestrian disciplines, e.g. eventing, showjumping, dressage, etc. Not only has the Thoroughbred been exported far and wide to improve racing stocks, it has also been used to improve hundreds of other breeds around the world.

All Thoroughbreds registered in the General Stud Book, started in 1791, can trace their pedigree back to the three Arabian foundation sires. Currently, Thoroughbreds are raced in over 50 countries of the world.

Descendants of the three foundation sires reached the United States in the 1730s, where they were generally similar to Thoroughbreds elsewhere; recently, however, a distinctive American type has emerged, with longer hindlegs and a longer stride, making its quarters appear higher in comparison.

The Thoroughbred is a beautiful and athletic animal, with long, clean limbs, a

The first Thoroughbred horse to reach colonial American was Bulle Rock, imported by Samuel Gist of Virginia in 1730.

fine, silky coat, an elegant profile and a muscular body. The eyes are always large and intelligent and the ears finely sculpted. Built for toughness, stamina and speed, the Thoroughbred is regarded as the ultimate racing machine.

Thoroughbreds are courageous, honest and bold, and one only has to be present at a steeplechase or hurdle race to see that this is so. The Thoroughbred is often described as 'hot-headed', and while this may be true of some individuals, which are more sensitive than others, most are a pleasure to own and ride.

Pure-bred and Thoroughbred are not synonymous in this context: the latter, in this case, is the actual name of this breed.

All true colors are acceptable, and height is usually between 15 and 16.2hh.

At once the coursers from the barrier bound;
The lifted scourges all at once resound;
Loose on their shoulders the long
manes reclined
Float in their speed, and dance upon
the wind.

Homer

211

TRAKEHNER

The Trakehner is the most elegant of the warmbloods and is the nearest in character to the Thoroughbred. Nowadays, because of its athleticism and paces, it is predominantly used for competition, particularly dressage and eventing.

The Trakehner has had a checkered history dating to 1732, when the first Trakehner stud was founded in East Prussia, part of the former kingdom of Prussia and now in Poland. The stud became the main source of stallions for the whole of Prussia and the area quickly became famous for its beautiful and elegant coach horses.

The breed came into being when native horses of the region were bred with Thoroughbreds and Arabs, infusions which gave the Trakehner its speed and endurance. Within 50 years, however, the emphasis had shifted from producing coach horses to breeding chargers for the cavalry, which

The neck and shoulders are shapely, the back short and strong and the quarters powerful. The legs are strong and straight, producing a powerful, straight action.

The Trakehner has an excellent temperament, being amiable, obedient and courageous. Although it resembles the Thoroughbred, it is without the 'hot' temperament associated with that breed. For this reason, breeders looking for an infusion of Thoroughbred without this trait often select Trakehner stallions instead.

All solid colors are acceptable and height is usually around 16–16.2hh.

continued until the Second World War, when the Trakehner stud was completely destroyed. Fortunately, towards the end of the war, about 1,000 horses were saved when they were trekked west, accompanied by refugees escaping from the Russian invasion. Although some of the horses died on the way, due to the harsh conditions, sufficient survived to continue the breed. Today, the breeding of the Trakehner is again flourishing in its place of origin, as well as in other countries.

In terms of appearance, the Trakehner resembles the middleweight Thoroughbred. The head is fine, with an intelligent and interested expression. The profile is straight and similar to that of the Thoroughbred.

The Trakehner is the purest of the warmblood breeds; this is because it has a closed stud book.

THE WELSH BREEDS

Horses were present in Wales as much as 10,000 years ago. At that time, the indigenous breed inhabiting the hills was the Celtic Pony, and it is thought that all Welsh breeds known today derive from this ancient breed.

It is recorded that native stock was being bred in Wales in around 50 BC, when Julius Caesar founded a stud in Merionethshire and was responsible for introducing Arab blood into the breed. The first mention of Welsh ponies and cobs appears in the laws of Hywel Dda, written in AD 930.

Throughout the centuries, variations on the original wild ponies were developed. Early on in the 20th century, the Welsh

Pony and Cob Society identified the four clear types described below. These are the original, once wild, Welsh Mountain Pony not exceeding 12hh (Section A); the Welsh Pony not exceeding 13hh (Section B); the Welsh Pony of Cob Type up to 13.2hh (Section C); the Welsh Cob of 13.2–15.2hh (Section D).

The Welsh Mountain Pony (Section A) is the oldest of all the Welsh breeds. As the name suggests it is tough, resilient, sound in limb as well as constitution. Known for its intelligence, agility, endurance and hardiness, the Welsh Mountain Pony is capable of surviving the harshest of winters. These ponies are now found all over the world and are highly regarded as quality children's riding ponies; they also perform well in harness.

THIS PAGE & OPPOSITE: Welsh Mountain Ponies are excellent all-rounders.

PAGES 216–217: A Section D Welsh Cob.

The head is refined, with a slim tapering muzzle and small, pricked ears. The eyes are large and bold. These qualities, as well as a dished face, give the Welsh Mountain a distinct resemblance to the Arab, a breed that has been introduced. The neck, well-defined withers and quarters are in proportion to the rest of the pony's body, while the tail is set quite high. The limbs are set square, with well-made joints, and the feet are small, rounded and hard.

The Welsh Mountain has great personality and charm, having inherited intelligence and quick-wittedness – traits which the original wild ponies seemed to have possessed in abundance. When in action, the gaits should be smooth and the hocks well-flexed.

They are usually gray, but all true colors are acceptable.

The Welsh Pony (Section B) has all the best attributes of the Welsh Mountain Pony, though breeders have accentuated its talents as a riding pony. Moreover, because the Welsh Pony has been used for generations on farms for herding sheep, it has similar toughness and agility.

These qualities, when combined with good looks, jumping ability, and superb conformation for riding, makes them perfect as children's mounts.

The Welsh Pony shares many similarities with the Welsh Mountain Pony. The head is refined, with small pricked ears, and the face may be slightly dished. The eyes are large and intelligent. The neck, back and quarters are muscular and in proportion, and the tail is set high. The limbs are straight and strong and the hooves strong and rounded.

The Welsh Pony is willing, active and enthusiastic and will always give of its best. Like the Welsh Mountain they are predominantly gray, but all true colors are acceptable.

The Welsh Pony of Cob Type (Section C) was originally used for farm work – also for carting slate from the mines. It is of a similar height to the Welsh Pony, but sturdier and capable of carrying heavier loads. It was developed more as a harness pony than for ridden work and has a naturally pronounced action, probably inherited from the Hackney, which was introduced into the breed.

General appearance is of a small cob. The eyes are spaced widely apart and the expression is intelligent. Like the others, the ears are small and pricked. The body and legs are sturdier and more cob-like than those of the Welsh Pony, and the feet are slightly larger. Mane and tail are full.

The Welsh Pony of Cob Type is similar in temperament to the other Welsh breeds, being lively and enthusiastic. It performs well in harness and is also a natural jumper.

All true colors are acceptable, but for the show ring, ponies are preferred with plenty of white on the lower legs.

Of all the Welsh breeds, the Welsh Cob (Section D) is the most famous. Known for its handsome appearance and extravagant paces, not only is it the ultimate working cob, it is also guaranteed to command attention in the show ring.

The breed dates to the 11th century, when it was known as the Powys Cob or Powys Rouncy. Welsh Cobs not only

possess Welsh Mountain Pony blood, they were also influenced by imports from all over the Roman Empire. Breeds from Spain, such as the Andalusian, and the Barb and Arab from North Africa, were all crossed with the early Welsh Cob variety. Later in the 18th and 19th centuries other breeds, such as Hackney and Yorkshire Coach Horse, were also introduced.

The Welsh Pony and Cob Society was formed in 1901, with the first stud book arriving the following year. The four sections into which the Welsh breeds are divided (ABCD) were specified in 1949.

Welsh Cobs were traditionally used by the military as well as by farmers, but they were so versatile that they could be used by virtually anyone needing transport or light haulage.

The Welsh Cob is compact, well-muscled, well-balanced and strong. It has a fine head with large, intelligent eyes and the usual small, pricked ears. The neck is arched and muscular, the back is short-coupled for strength, and the quarters are powerful and rounded. The legs are sturdy and straight and the hard and rounded feet are in proportion with the animal's body.

The Welsh Cob is proud, courageous, and extravagant in action. It is suitable for all disciplines and for all riders.

All true colors are acceptable.

WESTPHALIAN

Like most European warmbloods, the Westphalian is based on an older, heavier breed which had been native to Westphalia for hundreds of years. This native coldblood was crossed with Thoroughbred to produce a warmblood, which was first registered as a Westphalian in 1826, when the stud book was opened.

For many years, the horse was used for riding and light carriage work until measures were taken to improve the breed at the end of the Second World War. To improve its speed and endurance, as well as its intelligence, Westphalian stock was infused with more Thoroughbred and Arab blood, while Hanoverian was also added to ensure good sense and obedience.

The result was a riding horse of superb quality, which received its true recognition as a competition horse, particularly in showjumping, in the 1970s. Nowadays it not only excels at dressage but also at eventing.

The head is handsome and broad, with medium- to wide-apart ears, a straight nose and clever eyes. The neck is long and well-developed, with fairly prominent withers, a straight back, strong loins and well-muscled quarters. The shoulders are sloping, with a broad chest and deep girth. The legs are well-porportioned and strong with plenty of bone.

The Westaphalian is well-known for its courage and spirit. It is also obedient and easy to handle.

All solid colors are permitted, with white on the lower legs and head. Height is between 15.2 and 16.2hh.

The Westphalian is a quality horse, used for showjumping, dressage and eventing.

The Akhal-Teke appears to break almost every rule of good conformation. Its head is carried high on a long, thin neck set at an angle of 45 degrees to the body, giving it a proud, slightly haughty appearance. It has a fine, elegant head with wide cheeks and a straight or slightly dished nose; the large eyes are bold and expressive. The nostrils are dry and flared and the ears shapely and alert. Although the shoulders are broad and sloping, the chest is quite narrow. The body is fairly short, rounded and shallow, and the long loins have little definition. The girth is quite narrow, and the very long legs appear disproportionately long in relation to the body, and taper to small hooves.

It has an unusually smooth-flowing and powerful action. The shape of the pasterns are unique to the breed, possibly developed from negotiating desert terrain.

The Akhal-Teke is not known for its sunny nature, in fact, quite the reverse. It is willful and rebellious and benefits from one firm handler which it can learn to trust. It is an intelligent animal which requires careful and sympathetic training; it does not respond well to punishment and may very well retaliate. Due to its genetic inheritance it is unlikely to flourish cooped up in a stable and must be allowed a predominantly outdoor life, with plenty of space to wander.

Colors may be chestnut, bay, gray, palomino, black and dun. All the colors, apart from raven black, are strikingly iridescent. Height is approximately 15.2hh, though, with its pronounced withers and high head-carriage, the horse appears taller.

ARABIAN

The Arabian (Arab) is one of the oldest of the hotblooded breeds, and its bloodlines are present in many modern breeds found throughout Europe and the United States. The name is not strictly accurate, as the original 'Arab' may well have been a small Oriental-type wild horse, living in Eastern Europe, the Near East and the Middle East. The Arab was further developed as Islam assimilated the breed, and Muslim invaders used it as a cavalry horse. Today's modern Arabians can trace their descent from five foundation mares, known as Al-Khamesh (The Five), said to have been selected for their obedience.

And God took a handful of southerly wind, blew His breath over it, and created the horse.... Thou shall fly without wings, and conquer without any sword.....

Bedouin legend

The Arab was also of great importance to the Bedouin, the nomadic tribe of the desert, who can trace their association with the breed to 3000 BC, to the mare Baz and the stallion Hoshaba.

Arab horses were so-named when they were imported from the Arabian Peninsula to Britain in the 19th century. The Arab is also the foundation of the Thoroughbred. Arab blood is therefore highly effective when mixed with other breeds, and usually brings great improvements to any offspring that result.

Arabs are extremely beautiful, with a delicacy that belies their strength and

Bedouin breeders carefully recorded bloodlines and jealously guarded the purity of their horses. As a result, today's Arabians are as immediately recognizable as ever.

stamina. They shine in riding events, such as dressage, riding horse, and in-hand showing. They also excel in disciplines that rely on strength, such as endurance riding and racing. Arabs have the reputation of being unable to jump, which is quite untrue; they are keen jumpers, but lack the ability to compete at high level.

The head is short and refined, with a dish-shaped profile and a tapered muzzle with large nostrils. The eyes are large, wide-apart and low-set, and the ears are small, shapely and set well apart. The jaw is rounded and forms a curved arch where head and neck meet, known as the *mitbah*.

The back is slightly concave, with sloping shoulders and well-defined withers. The croup is level and the girth deep. The tail is set high. The legs are strong, hard and clean, with flat knees, short cannons, and well-defined tendons; the hooves are hard and tough. The Arab also has a distinctive skeletal feature, in that it has fewer vertebrae, i.e. 5 lumbar, 17 rib, and 16 tail, compared with 6-18-18 in other breeds, giving it a short-coupled appearance.

The horse's action is as if it were floating on air. Due to their desert origins

Nathan Harrison of Virginia imported the first Arabian stallion into North America in 1725. It reportedly sired 300 foals.

Arabs have a fine coat and skin which is designed to release heat. Consequently, they require special care in winter, though they are tougher than Thoroughbreds.

Arabs are famous for their intelligence and responsiveness. They are also affectionate and respectful of other animals, also of human beings, being especially good with children. The reverse side of their character is that they are fiery and courageous; they can also be stubborn if asked to do something against their will.

All solid colors are possible, but chestnut and gray are the most common. Arabs usually stand somewhere between 14 and 15.2hh.

CASPIAN

The Caspian is claimed to be the oldest breed of all and its history would seem to bear this out. It appears to have been descended from a prehistoric Oriental horse, and although domesticated, its bloodline has remained remarkably pure. Fossils of a prototype were found in Iran, which are almost an exact match of the bone structure of today's Caspian. A likeness of the horse can also be seen on a seal belonging to Darius the Great, who ruled Persia (Iran) in around 500 BC. The Caspian is probably the progenitor of the Arab Horse; consequently Caspian blood is in many of today's breeds.

It was thought that this small horse became extinct around the 10th century, so it was all the more amazing to discover a herd of 40, roaming in a remote region of the Elburz Mountains in 1965. These were shipped to England, where a breed society was established to preserve this rare and ancient breed; this was the start of studs being formed all over the world.

Nowadays, the Caspian's small stature makes it an ideal horse for children, and its equable temperament makes it particularly suitable for beginners.

The Caspian is typical of the Oriental type. The head is small and fine with small, alert ears and a straight nose with large nostrils. The eyes are large and intelligent. The neck is set quite high and is strong and elegant; the shoulders are sloping and the body is of medium proportions, even though it is quite narrow.

Although pony-like in size, the Caspian has the heart of a horse. It also has all the qualities needed to make it an excellent riding horse, being affectionate, intelligent and obedient. It has plenty of spirit, and also makes a good driving pony.

Caspians are usually bay, chestnut and gray. Height is in the region of 10–12hh.

The Caspian is said to be the oldest breed in the world, making it the possible prototype of the Arabian horse.

KATHIAWARI

Some are of the opinion that the original Kathiawari were descended from horses brought to India by Alexander the Great. Another theory is that they sprang from the wild horses of Kathiawari. However, the breed that was in evidence over 100 years ago was not a particularly attractive one, tending to be rather small and stunted as well as narrow in the body. It did, however, have assets that made it extremely useful: it was hardy, with amazing stamina and endurance, and had the ability to work all day with very little sustenance. It also had tough, hard feet, enabling it to cope with rough terrain.

This original stock was eventually enhanced by breeding with Arab, which greatly improved conformation. The breed is mainly to be found in the province of Gujarat, which comprises Rajkot, Bhavnagar, Surendranagar, Junagadh and Amreli.

The Kathiawari's most striking characteristic is its inward-pointing ears, which almost meet in the middle. The ears are also extremely mobile, and can rotate 180 degrees. The head is longish, with a slightly Roman nose; the forehead is broad, and the eyes are large and intelligent. Much of its Arab inheritance is immediately obvious: it is lightweight with fine legs, but has a predisposition to sickle hocks.

Kathiawaris come in most solid colors, most commonly chestnut, but bay, gray, dun, and colored horses are also possible. They stand between 14 and 15hh, depending on regional differences.

The Kathiawari is famous for its mobile ears. These can be rotated or even curved inward, almost joining in the middle.

MARWARI

The Marwari, from the Marwar region of Rajasthan, is similar in appearance to the Kathiawari, but is of much greater stature; it has often been featured in Indian art over the centuries. The Marwari is unusual in that it has a fifth gait, called the *revaal*, which is a long, smooth action with little vertical movement, which makes it very comfortable to ride.

Marwari numbers declined during the British occupancy of India, but thanks to today's Rajput families and others interested in the continuation of the breed, the Marwari is once again flourishing. It is now used as a dancing horse, popular at weddings and festivals. Their dance is a form of *haute école*, which the horse would have been taught when it was a warhorse long ago.

It has a high, proud head-carriage with a straight or Roman nose, its trademark ears curving inward until they almost join in the center. The eyes are large, bright and intelligent; the neck is of medium length

Traditional Rajasthani literature speaks highly of the Marwari's fabulous exploits, such as its ability to leap over high city walls.

and arches in movement. The coat is fine and silky. The Marwari has a naturally flamboyant presence and loves to perform, but it is also tough and able to survive harsh conditions. It is courageous, intelligent and a willing worker.

Marwaris may be any color, including roan, piebald and skewbald. They stand between 15 and 16hh.

PRZEWALSKI'S HORSE

This is a truly ancient breed, also known as the Mongolian or Asiatic Wild Horse. Primitive horses of this kind were hunted by man 20,000 years ago and the likenesses of similar horses can be seen in prehistoric cave paintings in Spain and France. No sightings of it have been made for over 30 years, so it is almost certainly extinct in the wild. It is the only true wild equine and the distant ancestor of the domestic horse.

The earliest written evidence of its existence was in the 9th century, and it was mentioned again in 1226, when a herd of wild horses are supposed to have caused Ghengis Khan, the founder of the Mongol Empire, to fall from his horse.

Because of its isolation and the fierceness with which stallions protect their mares, the Mongolian horse's bloodline has remained pure and can be traced back to its primitive ancestors.

It gets its modern name from the man who brought it to the attention of the world, Colonel N.M. Przewalski, a Polish explorer, who acquired the remains of a wild horse in 1881 from hunters who had discovered them in the Gobi Desert. He took them to the zoological museum in St. Petersburg, where naturalist I.S. Poliakoff examined them and decided that they belonged to a species of primitive wild

horse. Following the discovery, some of the living horses were captured and kept in captivity in zoos and wildlife parks so that they would be saved from total extinction.

The captive population has increased rapidly and is carefully monitored at Prague Zoo, which holds the stud book of the breed. The horses are kept in conditions that are as natural as possible; some have been released back into the wild in China, Russia and Mongolia, where they are a protected species, and a successful population can also be found in France.

The Przewalski is stocky, and has an erect, dark-brown mane. The head is of medium size, with a broad forehead and a straight or slightly dished nose. The wild-looking eyes are set high on the head and are rather small. The nose tapers to a narrow muzzle with small low-set nostrils. The body is strong, with a longish, straight back, a thick, short neck, and weak quarters. The legs are short and stocky with hard, tough hooves.

Przewalskis cannot be tamed and tend to be aggressive and ferocious, especially in the presence of their young. Being extremely hardy, they need very little extra attention.

Various shades of dun, ranging from yellow to red are possible. Przewalskis have black manes and tails and black legs, often with zebra markings, and there is a black dorsal stripe running down the back. The muzzle and the area around the eyes is a creamy-white color. They range in height from 12–14hh.

The Przewalski horse was hunted for centuries by the Chinese and Mongolians as a source of food, and the decline of the species was accelerated when firearms were eventually acquired.

HORSES OF AFRICA

BARB

The Barb has ancient origins, its name having been taken from a location in North Africa, once the fabled Barbary Coast, a section of the Mediterranean littoral stretching from Morocco to Egypt. Here, 2,000 years ago, cavalry horses were bred by Hannibal's Carthaginian forces.

At an early stage, the breed was probably influenced by the Arabian horse, brought to North Africa by the Arabs – also by hotblooded Oriental types. A great many were imported to Europe, particularly England, where many references to 'Barbary' horses are to be found, the most famous being Richard II's 'Roan Barbary'. Here they were also bred for the cavalry and

were prized for their speed and great stamina. Today it is difficult to find a pure-bred Barb. This is because of the widespread cross-breeding practised throughout the Mahgreb, its purpose being to produce good general riding horses.

The Barb is not a handsome horse and is inclined to be bad-tempered, but it has had a tremendous influence on other breeds,

particularly in Europe and the Americas. The Andalusian of Spain, the Connemara Pony of Ireland, the Thoroughbred, and even the Criollo of South America are all believed to have Barb blood in their veins.

Today the Barb is used for general riding, racing and display purposes. It remains very popular in its native land but receives little recognition elsewhere.

The Barb, bred for desert life, is fairly lightweight. The head is long and narrow, with a slightly dished face and medium well-shaped pointed ears; the eyes are kind and intelligent. The neck is of medium length, with a pronounced crest. The withers are prominent and the shoulders flat. The legs are fine, but strong, and the hooves are hard and well-shaped – a feature of all desert horses. The mane and tail are full, with the tail set low on flat quarters.

The Barb is quite stand-offish and inclined to be irritable. However, it has a reputation for extreme toughness, speed and stamina – qualities which have made it suitable for improving other breeds.

Most common colors are black, bay and dark brown, though Barbs with Arab blood can have coats of other colors, such as gray. The height range is 14.2–15.2hh.

The aim of the World Organization of the Barb Horse, founded in Algeria in 1987, is to preserve the breed, but it is difficult to say how its purity has been affected.

BASUTO

The Basuto, or Basotho Pony, is from Lesotho, previously Basutoland – an enclave of South Africa. The Basuto, bred mainly by the Bantu, was a development of the Cape Horse in the 19th century. By the early 20th century the breed had virtually disappeared, due to indiscriminate crossings with Thoroughbred, Indonesian and Spanish horses, in an effort to produce more substance.

The Basuto was eventually saved by a society established to improve and revive the breed in the later 20th century. In addition to the usual walk, trot and canter, the Basuto has two extra gaits, known as the triple and the pace.

The head is rather large, with an underdeveloped, shortish neck. The body and legs are strong and wiry, with hard hooves. Recent breeding programs have improved the Basuto, however, and the neck is now more shapely and the head finer.

The Basuto is tough and can survive adverse conditions on very little food and water. It is sure-footed, fast and fearless. It is only used for riding, as all draft work in Lesotho is done by cattle.

They come in all colors, as well as gray, and their height is usually around 14.1hh.

A chain of development, starting with the Cape Horse, created both the Basuto (below and opposite) and the Nooitgedachter.

BOERPERD

The Boerperd or Boer Horse, has a history that runs side by side with the white settlers of South Africa and the arrival of the Dutch in Cape Town in 1652.

The first horses seen in the region were of Oriental blood and were imported from Java, which in turn were sold by the Dutch East India Company to the Free Burghers in 1665. Over the years, however, significant inbreeding had taken place and measures were taken to improve the breed by introducing Arabian blood to the stock.

This practice continued for 150 years until a definite type emerged, known as the Cape Horse. Meanwhile, some Iberian breeds arrived in the Cape in 1793, which may or may not have had an effect on the native horses. In the late 18th and early 19th centuries, Cape Horses remained very popular and were prized for their endurance, stamina, speed and intelligence, which made them useful in a military role.

Over the years, various other influences affected the breed, and Flemish horses, Hackneys, Norfolk Trotters and Cleveland Bays brought further improvements. The breed continued to survive, despite disease and the Boer Wars, in which the horses certainly proved their worth.

The Boerperd (Afrikaans for farm horse) owes much of its appearance to its Oriental and Arab forebears. The head is small and wedge-shaped, with a slightly dished or straight nose, and it has a small, neat muzzle with flared nostrils. The eyes are bright and intelligent and the ears are medium-sized and alert. The body is short and compact, with a neatly sloping shoulder, deep girth, and well-proportioned muscular legs with plenty of bone. The hooves are tough and shapely.

The Boerperd is spirited, courageous and intelligent, with plenty of stamina and agility. They come in most solid colors and gray, and range from 14.2–15.2hh in height.

The history of the Boer Horse runs parallel with that of the white settlers in South Africa.

CHAPTER FIVE

HORSES OF AUSTRALIA

AUSTRALIAN PONY

During the colonization of Australia, many horses were imported and became an important part of Australian life. Ponies were also imported, but failed to attract any particular attention until the late 19th century, when a breed type began to emerge. By the 1920s the breed was starting to be recognized, and a stud book was eventually opened.

The Australian Pony is a combination of many breeds – Welsh, Thoroughbred,

Arab, Shetland and Exmoor, to name but a few. These are now so intermingled that no single characteristic is uppermost, apart, perhaps, from the Welsh and Arab influences, which can be seen in the fine head and neat legs. The result is an excellent all-rounder – good at jumping but dependable enough to be ridden by children; it is also perfect for trail-riding and endurance events.

The pony's most striking feature is its head, that makes its Arab ancestry

The Australian Pony Stud Book Society was formed in 1931. Today, the ponies are used in dressage, eventing and showjumping.

unmistakable. The ears are spaced well apart and are short and well-shaped; the forehead is broad and the eyes are large and kindly; the nose is slightly concave, with slightly flared nostrils leading down to a fine muzzle. The neck is well-developed with a silky, flowing mane; the withers are fairly pronounced and flow into a longish back with well-developed quarters; the legs are fine and tapered with strong tendons and short cannons, and the hooves are hard and shapely.

The Australian Pony is fairly lightweight and its hotblood ancestry is immediately obvious. It is, however, extremely hardy and has plenty of stamina.

Let us ride together, blowing mane and hair, careless of the weather, miles ahead of care, ring of hoof and snaffle, swing of waist and hip, trotting down the twisted road with the world let slip.

Anon.

The pony is known for its sound constitution, which makes it easy to care for and ideal for children, being also good-natured and obedient. Its most striking attribute is its free-flowing action.

The Australian Pony may be any color, with white on the head and legs but not on the body. Height is in the region of 12–14hh.

AUSTRALIAN STOCK HORSE

The Australian Stock Horse, otherwise known as the Waler, has a history that began in the 18th century, when horses were imported into Australia from South Africa and Chile. These tended to have excellent constitutions, being descended not only from Iberian, Arab, Barb, Criollo and Basuto stock, but also from Indonesian ponies. The quality of the first horses was found wanting, however, but later infusions of Arab and Thoroughbred brought great improvements to the stock.

The breed, also known as the New South Wales Horse, was once important as a cavalry horse. It was used by the British in India from about 1850, but soon became

The Waler was one of the finest cavalry horses in the world, used in the Indian Mutiny, the Boer Wars and First World War.

popular with stockmen, who saw its soundness and endurance as distinct assets in the huge expanses of the Australian outback; it was also used in harness.

By the 1940s, the Waler, as it was now generally known, had become a quality horse, but after the Second World War the population was allowed to dwindle. It was also bred with other horses, which subsequently weakened the breed. Today, steps are being taken to improve the Waler by adding Quarter Horse, Arab and Thoroughbred, but it has yet to be regarded as a consistent breed.

The ideal Waler has a fine head with a broad forehead, straight nose, and medium-length alert ears. The eyes are kind but inquisitive and intelligent. The neck is long and elegant with a slight crest, and the shoulders are sloping. The chest is broad with a deep girth, while the body is of medium length with strong loins and well-developed quarters. The legs are strong with shapely hooves.

The Waler has many excellent qualities. It is obedient and willing to work and is kind and intelligent. They are most often bays, though all solid colors are possible. They stand between 15 and 16.2hh.

BRUMBY

Australia had no native horses of its own until they were introduced during the country's gradual colonization, and in particular by settlers, who arrived during the 19th-century gold rush. Not only was there an influx of people, therefore, but also a large intake of horses and other animals.

During the First World War, many of the horses escaped or were turned loose to run wild: these were the forefathers of the modern-day Brumby, a name said to have been derived from the aboriginal word for wild (*baroomby*).

Because of the variety of animals that reverted to a wild state, there is no specific breed type; consequently Brumbies come in all shapes, sizes and colors.

The horses are now almost totally feral, making them difficult to catch and almost impossible to train. They are prolific breeders and for this reason have come to be regarded as pests. This has led to such extensive culling that they are now quite rare. They come in all colors and patterns. Height is up to 15hh.

Reminiscent of the American Mustang, there are more horses in the wild in Australia than in any other country in the world.

INDEX